ENDORSEMENTS

I thank the Prime Minister for his encouragement and support.

Honorable Prime Minister of India Mr. Narendra Modi signs the manuscript of #college

"*#college* throws up valuable advice for a student through the various sketches of Neha's experiences at a university that changed my life. A delightful book that vividly describes the excitement of studying at the University of Chicago - the fun, the rigour, the friends, the professors and the food! This is a must-read for anyone interested in knowing how a liberal arts education, not just at UChicago, can open your mind and help you discover yourself."

Luis Miranda
Chairman, Centre for Civil Society
MBA, Chicago Booth

"I loved it.
An absolute must-read for every student and surely for parents. It made me smile, laugh and moved me a little as I imagined my eight year old embarking on a journey like Neha's.

Apart from this, *#college* also compelled me to reflect upon my life, giving me pointers to redefine myself which is something we all need to do from time to time. Thanks, Neha!"

Sharman Joshi
Bollywood Actor

Seven Guidelines to
Define Your Success Story

NEHA PREMJEE

Copyright © 2014 Neha Premjee.

All rights reserved. No part of this book may be used or reproduced by any means, graphic, electronic, or mechanical, including photocopying, recording, taping or by any information storage retrieval system without the written permission of the publisher except in the case of brief quotations embodied in critical articles and reviews.

Abbott Press books may be ordered through booksellers or by contacting:

Abbott Press
1663 Liberty Drive
Bloomington, IN 47403
www.abbottpress.com
Phone: 1-866-697-5310

Because of the dynamic nature of the Internet, any web addresses or links contained in this book may have changed since publication and may no longer be valid. The views expressed in this work are solely those of the author and do not necessarily reflect the views of the publisher, and the publisher hereby disclaims any responsibility for them.

Any people depicted in stock imagery provided by Thinkstock are models, and such images are being used for illustrative purposes only.
Certain stock imagery © Thinkstock.

ISBN: 978-1-4582-1768-4 (sc)
ISBN: 978-1-4582-1769-1 (e)

Library of Congress Control Number: 2014915166

Printed in the United States of America.

Abbott Press rev. date: 11/5/2014

Front Cover photo credit: Ms. Victoria Pacey.
Taken on the University of Chicago Quadrangle.

ABOUT THE AUTHOR

Neha Premjee graduated from the University of Chicago in 2013 with honors and a double major in International Studies and Public Policy Studies. Her undergraduate experiences included a study abroad program in Rome and extensive travel through a semester spent at sea, exploring seventeen countries. Mumbai-based Premjee currently works in the international business media space writing country intelligence reports in various primary sector industries around the world.

DEDICATION

For my beloved parents, Sophia and Karim.
    Mom, for burning your midnight oil to ignite your children; for believing in me the most.

    Dad, for guiding us with your inherent wisdom and inspiring me to be a better human being everyday.

    Above all, thank you both for the unconditional love.

FOREWORD

Contributed by: Skylar Frisch

I distinctly remember the first time I met Neha. Well, to be more exact, observed her. She was one of the last to stroll, (In Neha's case, strut) into the classroom on our first day, August 25, 2013. My peers, professor and I were taken aback by her poise. She sat at a table next to mine. It was almost as if I was too stunned to introduce myself. *What was wrong with me, this girl wasn't a cute boy.* Luckily, Neha took the initiative.

In between thick black locks, her face was fresh and inviting, revealing a mouth unafraid to unleash her voice: clear, crisp and expertly articulate. I admired but mostly wondered how Neha could speak both so precisely and effortlessly. *Was she some sort of a superhuman?* After four months of daily interaction, I can confidently confirm that yes, Neha is. She is that and so much more.

That day, I was instantly intrigued, intimidated, and excited by my sparkling classmate. I remember looking around our 18-person classroom, realizing that we represented, physically, the global classroom that defines the Semester At Sea study abroad program, on a smaller scale. In addition to American students and our professor, there was a Guatemalan, Mexican, Chinese, Egyptian, and our resident half-Indian, half-superwoman, Neha.

Our professor, Gregory Justice, created a unique classroom environment. No, it wasn't just because class took place overlooking the ocean, in which he would permit us to rush to the floor-to-ceiling windows should there be a whale, dolphins, or even a school of flying fish just outside. We bonded in a way unlike any other class I had attended, supporting each other as well as bouncing ideas off our different personalities, cultures, and nationalities.

In class, Neha was driven and accurate. She always knew the correct answer, always gave the most insightful advice, she simply was the epitome of one of those kids whose perfection would usually irk you. But for our class, it was the exact opposite. With Neha, it is impossible to get a negative vibe.

We would cheer her on as well as probe her with questions and inquire about her accomplishments. After only a few classes, she was everyone's go-to-- it was always "Hey Neha, could you take a look at this," "Let's get Neha's opinion," or something of the like. Her responses and guidance never let us down. In the presence of such a worldly, inspiring and cultured peer, Neha shook us out of our state of awe and into her mindset, which I can only describe as holistic grace—a combination of drive, confidence, genuineness, global perspective, and a healthy dose of dreaming.

While it often takes awhile to get to know someone, Neha's friendly demeanor and confidence make her one of the most warm and accepting people I've ever met. Her humor, not always intentional, left our class in stitches. Needless to say, once I got over my initial and brief intimidation of my flawless classmate, I found myself a true friend.

Neha and I became closer when we were placed in the same "Extended Family" group, which is a shipboard program which breaks students and faculty members into small groups in order to create a family environment away from home. Our "parents," a retired astronaut and his wife, provided us with plenty of food, including cake, ice cream, and that for thought. Following our family get-togethers, Neha and I would head up to the seventh deck, which stared out into the open blue ocean, and alternate between discussions about our "parents'" accomplishments and our own at great length, pausing to gaze up at the moon and the dazzling stars where our "Dad" had taken his space missions. Neha had recently spoken eloquently at the United Nations conference in Geneva but had shown me her other side, the one that raged at the Ultra Music Festival in Miami just a few months prior. She is one of the most balanced college students I have met, simultaneously achieving and daring to dream. Our oceanside table for two was the perfect setting for talking about our pasts and our plans for the future.

I was surprised to find that my seemingly perfect friend had experienced some bumps in the road. Even Neha had faced college rejection letters. Had her fair share of uncertainties. Experienced the culture shock of adjusting to college, which in her case, was in a country far from her home in Mumbai.

Maybe it was our similarities that made us click so well as friends. I admired how she had moved from Mumbai to Chicago to attend her dream university, just like she marveled at how I had left home at 14 years old to attend boarding school. I admired her polished look that she wasn't afraid to mess up with a run on the treadmill and sweatpants, while she admired my sportiness. We both love to joke. Her Mom is her best friend and so is mine. We both love adventure, and share a passion for travel. Hence the 16 countries we traveled to in that semester.

I am fortunate that Neha has already graduated from a top university, but since I am still in college, I will still get to take advantage of all she has learned and experienced. A junior at the University of Miami, I consider myself to have a pretty good handle on things: balancing schoolwork, a social life, my own passions, and a global perspective enriched by a recent study abroad experience. But if there is one thing I've learned from Neha, it is that there is a lot to learn-- from the world, from science, from nature, and from each other. I encourage readers to do what I will: look to her advice in this book to guide me as well as validate and empathize with what I have already experienced. Like Neha herself, it will also serve as inspiration.

If you think 23 years old sounds too young for someone to write an autobiography, you haven't met Neha. She may be only 3 years my senior, but she is my role model. She is a quick-witted friend I hold dear though she lives 7,605 miles away. I am confident that her maturity and insight will be invaluable to any collegiate career. As accomplished as she is, Neha maintains distinct qualities of relateability and humbleness. I am confident that her autobiography is one of many accomplishments to come.

Cheers to your past, your present, your future, and the spark you ignite in all those you meet, Neha!

Love always, your friend,
Skylar A. Frisch

PREFACE
November 2013

It is in human nature to reminisce and reflect back on an episode thinking, *I wish I could relive that experience with the knowledge that I gathered going through it.* As Vernon Law puts it, "Experience is a hard teacher because she gives the test first, the lesson afterward."

I graduated from the University of Chicago five months ago with two Bachelors of Arts and a similar set of musings. Through my time as an undergraduate I was given many tests – round after round of midterms and finals and the more challenging examinations of life whose lessons led me to leave college an older and (hopefully) wiser individual.

As my time at Chicago was nearing its end, my family flew down from India a week before the convocation ceremony. My younger brother Armaan, who anticipates starting college next year asked me an insightful lot of questions during a casual family dinner over deep dish pizza. "Knowing what you do today, if you could go back in time and start college again would you still choose the University of Chicago?" Yes, absolutely! I nodded my head vigorously as I bit into a cheesy slice pulling a thick string of mozzarella away from my face. This one was a no-brainer. The University of Chicago is one of the most prestigious institutions in the United States of America and what I learnt from the community of scholars, neighborhood and city is priceless. I wouldn't trade this experience in for anything. It wasn't just what I learned, but also the feelings and confidence with which I was stepping into the real world. I was enjoying a feeling of exhilaration, although I will admit that could have been due to the deep dish. Pizza has a way of inspiring a range of happy emotions, particularly in college students. In all seriousness, I was leaving my school having found my passion, admired and respected in the eyes of the people I cared about. Despite facing a fair share of challenges while navigating through the funky university ecosystem, I had made the most of my time while learning how to be happy and remain in love with my life. Leaving my beautiful school was the epitome of a bittersweet escapade, but it now felt more bitter as I didn't want to leave what had grown to taste so sweet.

Armaan proceeded, "What do you now know that you wish you knew four years ago?" I didn't quite know how to approach this question. Not because I didn't have anything to say, but because I had no clue where to begin. The trials and tribulations (from a collegiate's perspective, of course) I faced led me to amass a wealth of insights in diverse areas. I had comments on academics, extracurriculars, career pursuits. I had lessons to share about building a social life and my study abroad experience. Philosophies on how one should approach mundane activities and the overarching four years in general. As our topic of conversation at dinner was clearly centered on what I had gained in the last four years, I immediately began thinking about the things I wish I could go back in time and tell my freshman self. I wanted to answer Armaan's question honestly and thoughtfully, and prepare him with the tools to create the best college experience for himself. I replied that I had so much to say about what I learnt through my college experiences that I could write a book on the subject. And so was born #college.

***

If you're a high school junior, senior or even a college freshman, chances are you will encounter numerous platforms offering advice on how to best live one's life in a university environment. There are online pieces such as '10 things every college student should do' and articles that discuss experiences that should be had with academic experimentation, Greek life, dating and sex, alcohol, adjusting to changes in food and diet, not procrastinating, among other concerns. Despite the diversity of direction that exists in guiding students towards enlightenment, I've seen that people tend to absorb and apply what is most relevant to them. No two individuals will undergo the same set of occurrences. Upon reflection, I came to realize that there were seven defining, yet generic lessons that shaped me through my academic, extracurricular and study abroad experience in college. I valued these learnings only after having lived the experience and decided to share my story and the insights I gleaned. Although the mantras are simple, I believe that they aren't highlighted enough.

We have one life to live, so may as well make the most of it. The world has far too many dispassionate forty-something year olds that would give an arm and a leg to be twenty again, and with good reason. The transition from high school to undergraduate college is probably one of the most exciting shifts in one's life with the anticipation of a tremendous learning curve. Being seventeen or eighteen years of age and full of energy can create that nervous excitement and anticipation of what lies ahead. "What will my new life be like?" or "Will I be able to cope up with the rigors of college" are two of million questions that cross a typical high schoolers mind as he or she awaits the next big change in this wonderful journey of life. The mass of questions is understandable because undergraduate education at a university in the United States typically comes with numerous opportunities. The pressure of making the most of these in order to build identity capital can be overwhelming although it doesn't have to be a daunting task if one knows how to embrace the highs and learn from the lows. The following chapters are written for any student at the threshold of an undergraduate education desiring to maximize their experience while leading a balanced life through these influential years. I'm twenty-three years old, which means I'm too young to preach. Therefore, I've encapsulated my philosophies through personal stories, aiming the lens at the details of my own affairs. More nuanced than a simple college survival guide, I'm hoping my narrative will bring to surface the multiple, more subtle tensions one is likely to face over four years. But before thinking about the tensions and letting them cloud the sunshine that beckons, get ready for the best years of your life. I'm not alone when I say that these are the ultimate years filled with fun, interesting people, hard work, provoking conversation, adjustment, insanity, great times in a new world that will absolutely exhilarate you, if you let it.

CHAPTER 1

Graduating UChicago: College of the Phoenix, All Ends With Beginnings

"Life is the most exciting opportunity we have. But we have one shot. You graduate from college once, and that's it. You're going out of that nest. And you have to find that courage that's deep, deep, deep in there. Every step of the way."
- Andrew Shue

The true extent of my emotional attachment to the University of Chicago hit me as I sat amidst twenty thousand odd people on a sweltering, uncomfortable summer's day. It was the fifteenth day of June in 2013, the day of my graduation. The end of four action-packed, happening years of my life. Also a beginning full of promise. It was not an ideal time to be sitting layered in a long black robe for hours. Climatically, Chicago is reputed to be erratic. While winters last for well over half the year with sub-zero temperatures and a wind chill that often made my ears feel like they were going to explode, summers embodied a mercilessly scorching sun. Despite the heat, there were more tears sliding down my cheeks than beads of sweat trickling down the side of my face. I sat there in all my ceremonial regalia and cried. I did not want to leave.

My family and friends were in the parents' section a distance away with huge smiles plastered on their faces. Over the last few days they had been emphasizing how happy and proud I had made them. While everything I had accomplished during my four years at college did manage to thrill me, I was sad that my undergraduate phase in life had come to an end. I had developed a profound attachment for this university; campus had become my home, the people within it my family. I asked myself what had happened in these last four years that made me fall so deeply in love? The very place I had first walked into with feelings of unfamiliarity and uncertainty now inspired feelings of a strong bond that I wasn't ready to severe. My thoughts went back in time to 20th September 2009, when I first entered UChicago's portals as a budding freshman saying goodbye to my (then sobbing) parents at the location for the 'Rite of Passage', the historic Hull Gate. It is historic because as per UChicago tradition, this is where incoming students officially say goodbye to their families during O-week. Now, before you begin to wonder what exactly is celebrated during this week, it is the popular name for Orientation week, that is organized each year to familiarize newly admitted students and help them settle into college. O-week begins with a host of day-long activities for students and their families that enable them to get acquainted with the hundreds of extracurricular student organizations and other important locations on campus, such as the residence halls, libraries, dining halls and banks. Crossing over at Hull Gate represents transition. The ceremony of leaving one's parents at the gate symbolically reflects the act of saying goodbye to family in embracing a new pursuit of growth and learning. There is an elaborate bagpipe procession with melancholy harmonies further triggering the waterworks... some parents really cry while leaving their kids! They say experience is a great teacher and the University's many decades of experience was evident, as the authorities had thoughtfully stationed student volunteers at strategic spots who empathetically offered boxes of Kleenex to the parents. I have yet to see Kleenex being consumed as rapidly as I did that day. We students hugged and re-hugged our parents, said our tearful goodbyes and crossed Hull Gate into the campus. A few meters down the road, I was surprised to see a scene of total contrast - jubilation! Upper classmen were dressed in costumes, high-fiving the incoming freshmen. There was a celebratory atmosphere and the air was charged with excitement and good cheer. It was almost like a new life was waiting to happily embrace us.

For most people, college is a time to attain independence and realize what it means to be truly self-reliant. Being away from parents and family, you aren't answerable to anybody and nobody is answerable to you. You're on your own. You'll be faced with multiple choices, many of whose consequences will stretch far beyond those four short years. In her book and TED talk, prominent psychologist Dr. Meg Jay discusses the twenties as a developmental sweet-spot. She refers to it as the "defining decade" of one's life. Whether in the spheres of career or personal relationships, most pivotal life choices tend to be made in this timeframe. College offers a great opportunity to hone one's decision-making abilities – some fabulous and diverse resources, programs and experiences to gain the skills to make veracious choices that define one's present and future. Possessing this skill almost always leads to making the most of an opportunity when it presents itself.

I distinctly remember my own feelings when I first entered Hull Gate - I felt relatively emotionless and detached, taking in all the strange faces and scenes that surrounded me, and experienced a mildly nervous anticipation of what lay in store for me. Now the time had come to go up on stage, collect my degrees and walk back out through Hull Gate a graduate, where the world outside awaited. I felt sad to leave the place I had grown to love. The tables had turned: my parents were the cheerful ones, beaming happily from ear to ear (maybe part of it had to do with the fact that they would no longer have to pay my college bills) while I was the sad one now that it was time to leave college. I was flooded with a flurry of emotions that welled up as uncontrollable tears. I looked around me. Where were those Kleenex volunteers when you needed them most?

How was it possible to grow so attached to a place that once felt so alien? Was it specific incidents? Was it the people? The four years at college had exposed me to a range experiences that defined me academically, professionally and personally and made me feel like my time at this wonderful institution had been so worthwhile. The host of inspiring individuals I met had a deep impact and influence on me. As the speaker on stage began to elaborate on the significance of the day's events, I let my mind wander. I began to think about each and every facet of the life I had built for myself ....a flashback of my UChicago undergrad experience.

Academically, I had managed to pack in a great deal. All those long nights we students spent burning the midnight oil at the Regenstein Library before midterms or final examinations, seemed well worth it now. I was graduating with honors and a double major in International Studies and Public Policy Studies. This had been possible by cultivating important skills through my coursework and honors-winning bachelors thesis. Realizing my passion propelled me to fulfill my coursework two quarters earlier than most students, in December 2012. It was nice to have seven extra months to work, travel and relax before graduating with my class in June the following year.

I thought about the weeknights that I had filled with various extracurricular activities. UChicago, like most colleges in its league is rich with a rigorous curriculum, events and clubs. There are over four hundred Registered Student Organizations (RSOs) and I loved being an active and contributing member of my community. Wednesday evenings were invariably devoted to the UChicago Careers in Business Program, which hosted alumni and business leaders who delivered talks on the various facets of business. Hearing role-models helped me define the professional life I wanted to lead as an adult and the program provided me with the resources to move towards actualizing that vision. When I wasn't investing in my future, I served as a Career Peer Advisor, enjoyed throwing my hands up and dancing in the South Asian Students Association's annual show and held a beguiling part time job tutoring high school students. Frequently, there were talks and seminars I wanted to attend and pursuing a diversity of activities in addition to an active social life, I habitually felt the way one feels on cruise vacations: there is always something going on at all times. I wished my day had twenty-eight hours so that I could pack in more.

 My attention darted back to the graduation ceremony for a second, and I shifted in my seat as I wiped my sweat. My eyes scanned the quadrangle and I spotted my friend Matt. Despite my tears, he still managed to make me smile with his animated face and warm smile. He waved out to me and I waved back, recalling my study abroad experience in Rome earlier that year. Matt and I had got to know each other as he was dating one of my friends, but we became better acquainted during a three month-long Study Abroad stint in Rome. Apart from Matt, I made three other close friends from UChicago who were on the program - Ada, Lauren and Johnny. As part of my Civilization Studies requirement, I was fortunate to have the opportunity to spend an incredible quarter abroad studying Italian culture, art and history while eating the most delightful foods and gallivanting around Europe on weekends. We spent day in and day out exploring the Eternal City and grew so close during the time that it felt like I had started my Roman adventure with four friends and ended it with four family members. My eyes welled up again as thoughts of leaving them entered my mind. My face was now an unfortunately salty hodgepodge of sweat and tears. I got up to go wash my face in the gym and across the street from me was the Neighborhood Schools Program office. Tucked into the corner of 55th street and Ellis Avenue, the NSP office is where I spent many afternoons through my second, third and fourth years. It was strange to think that this was probably the last time I'd be seeing that office. I was chosen to work with the program and held a part time job tutoring high school students in the south side of Chicago. The hardworking staff at the office recruited college students to work in local schools that needed support, thereby helping fulfill an important educational need through community outreach. I was placed with an ambitious lot of high schoolers, many of who were from less privileged backgrounds and were to be the first in their families to attend college. Guiding them through the application essay writing process to ensure that they achieved their goals was one of my most rewarding experiences. There is a unique joy in being able to give back, no matter in how small a way.

As I walked passed a flurry of runners on the treadmills on my way to the bathroom, I thought about how much sweat people had to put into accomplishing their targets. I too had spent many hours on those treadmills as staying healthy was an important priority for me. Faulty eating habits as a freshman and a history of obesity through my teenage years led me to weigh one hundred and ninety six pounds at the end of my first year at college. That is a LOT of weight for a medium-framed five foot six inch girl. People had warned me about the "freshman fifteen", that is fifteen pounds of weight that the typical college freshman gains due to a change in environment. Sadly for me, the freshman fifteen turned out to be more like the freshman forty. I didn't exactly love my obese self. Not willing to accept my condition, I made eating right, running and practicing yoga a part of my daily life in an effort to become healthy and develop a positive self-image. I spent many days on those very treadmills, at times after long days in the classrooms and libraries. It thrills me to say that I graduated over fifty pounds lighter, at a normal weight thus enabling me to run the Mumbai Half Marathon in 2013 and then again in January 2014. Losing weight was a tremendous personal accomplishment that had a domino effect of positive consequences. I became a lot more confident, looked and therefore dressed better and changed my overall attitude. Achieving the balanced life I desired didn't come easy. I often felt overwhelmed attempting to pursue all my goals: good physical health, active participation in the community, aiming for stellar grades while pursuing a double major, career concerns and a great social life – but as they say, college is a time to develop important life skills and all of this multitasking allowed me to designate the college experience as 'the best years of my life'.

You're probably wondering how I managed to fit in the time to sleep through all of that. The truth is that despite being 22 years old, I'm probably closer to a 2 year old when it comes to sleep. I need 7-8 hours of quality time with my bed each night, and college was no exception. Apart from finals week, and the nights I was out clubbing on weekends, I managed to make it to bed at a pretty reasonable hour and possess a relatively healthy sleeping pattern. It took a lot of observing, making and fixing mistakes for me to arrive at a comfortably optimal balance.

On my trek back to my seat, thoughts on academic, health and personal success flooded my mind all at once. Like most of the young graduates on those chairs, I had managed to pack in quite a bit. My foundational takeaway from key experiences such as completing a double major early, losing weight or studying abroad is the importance of preparedness. Without thoroughly planning each of these out, I probably wouldn't have achieved my targets. Although my mind fixated over my achievements on paper, my heart felt for all the incredible moments that made it all worthwhile. How did my thinking and approach to life change as I navigated through the multitude of opportunities? More importantly, how I did manage to stay happy and balanced through it all? Let me start my story at the beginning, before I even got to university.

CHAPTER 2

"You Can't Sit With Us"

"The size of your dreams must always exceed your current capacity to achieve them. If your dreams do not scare you, they are not big enough."
- Ellen Johnson Sirleaf

Even the most accomplished individual, at some point in their life, has been doubted. Being told "you can't" or "that's impossible" is a negative, confidence-shattering feeling that leaves one questioning their self worth. People tend to judge others' capabilities and place them in categories accordingly. How many times have you heard the phrases, "She's out of your league" or "There's no way you can do that"?

The dominating, popular female high schoolers in the film *'Mean Girls'* use a compelling phrase that I've seen have implications in real life. One of the characters tells her friend at lunch, "You can't sit with us" thereby dictating and imposing a value upon her friend. This has been defined by Urban Dictionary as "The phrase that you say to people if they try to sit at the plastic's lunch table while wearing track pants on a day that isn't Friday or a pony tail for the second time in a week or a color other than pink on Wednesday. *That's against the rules and YOU CAN'T SIT WITH US!"* Although not everybody has mean girls in their lives telling them where they can or can't sit and the average person's considerations extend to issues deeper than what clothing or hairstyle to sport, the game of life is nonetheless filled with dictators and rules. I was a senior in high school when I first recollect experiencing the harshness of judgment. A reputed American university was a lunch table that I wanted to sit at for my undergraduate life, and many people along the way told me - you guessed it - that I couldn't sit there. It was a dream way out of my league. I apparently didn't fit the stereotype of an academic high-achiever. Here is how I went about breaking that stereotype.

I was born and raised in Mumbai, India. Mumbai is a vivacious, bustling metropolis of sharp contrasts. The city's coastline opens up to the vast expanse of the Arabian Sea, while the congested landscape houses over 18 million people. The concrete skyscrapers stand juxtaposed against a dense concentration of slums. At traffic lights, it is not uncommon to see a beautifully attired socialite roll down the window of her chauffeur-driven Mercedes, her impeccably manicured hands groping in the depths of her limited edition Louis Vuitton to gather some loose change that will buy a meal for the beggar child who has been waiting all day, approaching car after car that stops at the traffic light, for some generosity. Despite the evident social dichotomy, I love Mumbai. There is something about the character of this pulsating city that is hard to explain. There is a unique resilience about Mumbaikars, as the residents are called. Be it bouncing back from the terrorist attack on the city in November 2008 or the floods which left the city crippled in July 2005, folks demonstrate a high willingness to help each other and recover from setbacks. Poverty notwithstanding, it is a relatively safe city that is inclusive enough to serve as a melting pot of the diverse people from all regions of India and other parts of the world who choose to make it their home. Being a communal culture helps people stay happy and rally together in tough times. I attended Ecole Mondiale World School, a private, international school situated in Mumbai's elite suburb, Juhu. I knew that receiving a quality college education in the United States of America would require me to jump a few hurdles – apart from applying to a number of colleges and getting accepted which is the universal challenge for any aspiring student and convincing myself that I had aptly narrowed down the best-fit schools for myself, it also entailed convincing my parents, grandparents, aunts, uncles, grand aunts, grand uncles other concerned family members and the odd inquisitive neighbor that I should indeed be sent abroad. The general sentiment was that perfectly good undergraduate education is available in India as well, so why travel so far away from home? Now, in general, Indians tend to adopt a collectivist approach to decision making in most facets of one's life – families are by and large, close knit. Decisions impacting an individual are influenced by the opinions of multiple stakeholders. So, it was rather amusing to observe the range of reactions I got when I first announced that I was interested in going to America for undergraduate education:

My father: How much is this going to cost?

My mother: This is great! I am delighted that you are aspiring for good things for yourself.

My *Dadi* (paternal grandmother): I will miss you and your resounding laughter that lights up our home. Please eat well and let me teach you to cook the things you like to eat.

My *Nani* (maternal grandmother): I hope you will stay away from bad influences. Stay away from alcohol and drugs. Stay away from cigarettes. Stay away from lecherous boys. Stay in close touch with us.

My *Nana* (maternal grandfather, a very meticulous person who pays great attention to detail): Where will you go? Is it safe? How will you live all by yourself? What if you get sick? Who will take care of you? How will you transport yourself from the airport to whichever campus you choose?

My building neighbor (to my parents): Now what is the need to send a child so far away to study? Don't we have good colleges right here in Mumbai?

My aunt (to my parents): Please be very, very careful and cautious before taking such an extreme step. She may forget her roots and choose to marry a foreigner!

Needless to say, I had to adopt rather different strategies and arguments to convince each one.

Getting accepted into college is a process in itself. It requires test-taking and essay writing, and presenting one's best self in a few meager pages of an application form – it isn't exactly a walk in the park. Furthermore, what confounds the process is the precarious game of balancing lofty aims with being realistic in evaluating one's accomplishments. SAT scores, school grades, recommendations, extracurriculars and essays are all to be considered when determining one's worth so there can be variations and subjectivity in defining which "league" an applicant falls in. Oftentimes it is easiest to go with numerical criteria, as they are definite so applicants are (mistakenly) told where they stand based on standardized test scores and grade point averages. I too happened to be a victim of this phenomenon. The truth is, with the exception of those with the perfect score of 2400, most high school students tend to be so. We obsess over the SAT score and no matter how well we have done, feel that we can do better given another attempt just so we can match up or stand out.

After researching several schools and their various programs I decided that I wanted to attend a premier university, and most schools that I shortlisted also happened to be top-10 undergraduate institutions according to the US News rankings. Making my dreams come true would be a progression, but that required me to first dream and outline an ambitious vision for myself. I've always believed that visualizing success is like planting the seeds towards maximizing one's potential. While hard work and determination serve as water and sunshine, dreaming is the first step towards attaining new paradigms. This however often requires progressing past set or socially imposed boundaries. The first boundary I had to break through was a tough one - apparently me, and my relatively low SAT score were well below the 'UChicago league'. Upon surfing websites of colleges I was interested in applying to, I discovered that the average SAT scores for admitted students in the previous year was about 2200. My best score after two attempts was 1980. It wasn't that I didn't study for the test. Frankly, I simply wasn't a naturally gifted standardized test taker. To compound this challenge was the fact that the education system in India isn't geared to preparing students for the SAT. Prior to enrolling in an international high school, I spent elementary and middle school learning in the Indian educational system where the pedagogical focus was centered on getting students to memorize and retain information from content-heavy texts to enable them to answer examination papers. Skills like research, analysis, evaluation and a variety of presentation styles were compromised for imparting or transferring information from teacher to student. As my primary education didn't focus on cultivating adeptness at critical reading, writing and logical reasoning which are tested on the SAT, I was at a disadvantage. I must admit though, that while a few Indian students do manage impressive scores at the SAT despite the education system, by and large most Indian students find the SAT a challenge and in general there have been endeavors to bring about a transformation in the nation's educational system through a re-look at the policy, spreading awareness through films and various other media. One of my all-time favorite Bollywood films, the critically acclaimed

'3 *Idiots*' highlighted this phenomenon of the enormous pressure on young students to obtain high scores and the futility of excessive focus on academic achievement being linked to later success in life. Anyway, experienced voices warned me that the scores I had achieved didn't quite correspond to my dreams. I was told that it was very difficult to gain admission to the highly competitive schools I wanted to attend and that I should be more realistic in my choices. Despite my self-confidence getting a tad bit deflated, I knew in my heart that my SAT scores didn't accurately reflect my academic ability. I sought solace in a quote that I had heard: "They say there are three kinds of lies in the world – lies, damn lies and statistics." I desperately hoped that the college admissions officer would scratch below the surface, look beyond the numerical façade, look past the lies contained in my score and see the real me.

October 2008 loomed around and hundreds of thousands of twelfth graders in my city began considering their futures. Mumbai being one of the most populated cities in the world, there are always too many people vying for limited facilities of good standard, be it health care, education or transportation. At times the situation is akin to hundreds of hungry sharks fighting for a prized prey. Unlike the average cut-throat and highly competitive environment in most Mumbai schools, my high school, Ecole Mondiale, fostered an extremely nurturing environment. Our class size was relatively small; we had a favorable student - teacher ratio ensuring that each student had opportunities to interact and contribute in class. There were multiple openings to lead, serve and get involved. Faculty too was devoted and did their best to ensure that students succeeded in the International Baccalaureate (I.B.) examinations. Our college counsellor, Ms. Leena Francis took great pains to understand each student's individual needs and goals. She provided us with various tools to help us understand ourselves better, administered the Myers-Briggs Type Indicator test, and sent home questionnaires for our parents asking them to describe their child and events in childhood that may have shaped us. She extended herself to write favorable yet accurate, descriptive recommendations (or so I think!) and provided well-meaning advice to children that took the initiative to follow up with her with respect to their college applications.

Ms. Leena Francis's office is appropriately nestled on the third floor of the Ecole Mondiale World School building, surrounded by glossy and inviting posters of university campuses located around the world from the USA, UK, Singapore, Canada and Australia. I was outside her office one afternoon and it was now my turn to meet her for a one-on-one appointment to shortlist the colleges I would be applying to.

"Neha, you have a score of 1980, and your college application list reads UPenn, Brown, Duke, Cornell, Columbia, University of Chicago, etc. Perhaps you'd want to cut out a few of these schools and include more...er, realistic choices? Based on the scores, a typical student applies to 2-3 dream schools, 5-6 target schools and 2-3 safety options. In my opinion you've got 9 dreams, 2 targets and 0 safeties."

I slumped down in my seat as it dawned upon me that the counselor basically suggested I quit dreaming. I realized that in her wisdom and experience she was attempting to protect me from the disappointment of facing multiple rejections; yet, I couldn't help but feel pricked. People like me that are dreamers often tend to be extra sensitive to reality checks like the one Ms. Francis had just pitched at me. I tried to console myself by saying that I could always take the test again, perhaps perform better? I still felt insecure, and thought, "Am I overestimating myself? What if I'm genuinely not as good as I believe myself to be?"

Having grown up in the Indian City of Dreams, home to the 3 billion-dollar movie industry popularly known as Bollywood (coined by conjoining Bombay to Hollywood), reading about and watching television shows that glamorize the prestige of attending an Ivy League institution, I'd spent a large portion of my high-school life aspiring to attend an academically rigorous top school in the United States of America. I invested much time and energy working hard in classes and pursuing activities that would help me actualize my goals, and now my standardized test scores were staring at me in the face as a rejection in advance. Ms. Francis looked at me as if I had suggested that I wanted to go on a date with Brad Pitt, Johnny Depp or Tom Cruise...why bother trying?

"Don't get me wrong," she said when she saw that her words had dejected me. "You're a fantastic student - you have impressive grades, and you've been an involved leader in school. I'm sure you are going to attend a very good school, and we're going to help you get there but I don't understand your obsession with these so-called top schools.

Why don't you consider the smaller, liberal arts colleges? I honestly think you'd make a wonderful fit at any of these places and they tend to really nurture a student with all the individual attention one gets in classes. They are excellent schools to facilitate personal growth. Here! Read these brochures and perhaps you can come back to me next week with a revised list."

I went home and read through the brochures. I looked at the academic profiles and philosophies of the colleges my counselor was suggesting I applied to. They all seemed like acclaimed places to pursue an education, but they simply did not excite me. I always dreamt of being in a large University campus. I could not envision myself at one of the smaller schools, no matter how hard I tried to convince myself that applying to them would be the "realistic" thing to do. I was also very clear about the fact that choosing a college was like choosing a husband: it had to excite me! After all, I was going to leave home and family behind and travel thousands of miles to attend college; the substantial financial investment that would be incurred no matter which school I attended, so why shouldn't it be the one I perceived as best for myself?

In times of doubt, my mother is my first go-to person. Although an eternal optimist like me, Sophie possesses excellent judgment, knows how to present a balanced perspective and offer sensible advice. I'm quite fond of my mother and like most parents she takes a lot of pride in her children. Listening to her is delightful because she is always telling me how awesome I am, and I could have really used the ego boost that evening.

"Mom, I'm confused," I said as our family sat down to dinner later at night. "I'm not sure whether I should cut out some of the top schools on my college application list or retain them. The counselor thinks I should replace them with schools that are ranked, well, not in the US News Top 10. My SAT score is relatively poor, and I've heard that applications below 2100 aren't even considered."

Sophie frowned. "Now why on earth would you do that? You're a bright, enthusiastic girl who deserves the best." Bingo. She always knows just what to say to me.

I smiled back in an effort and gently explained, "Mom, it's great that you think I deserve to be there but that doesn't really mean I'm getting in. If you were on the admissions committee at one of these schools, believe me I would apply with no hesitation."

And without any hesitation, she replied, "Neha, I honestly believe you're going to go to a top school. I think you'll end up in a place that'll match your personality, facilitate your growth and allow you to be a contributing member of its community. A standardized test score doesn't determine this match. Everybody has a score, but what'll set you apart is what you've done in school, how you've challenged yourself and how well you present yourself in your essays. I'd much rather you apply to all the top schools, and the smaller liberal arts ones too if you want to cast your safety net wide. After all, what does it take? 70 odd dollars in application fees, a few hours writing the essays and the courage to face a possible rejection letter. Just do it. In contrast, look at what do you stand to gain - who knows where you could land up!"

"You should just apply everywhere," my dad, the supportive realist, chimed in. "Its nice to have high hopes, but you also want to secure yourself. Remember, when you reach for the stars you might not touch them but you'll probably land up somewhere in the sky." That was typical advice you'd expect from my dad. He is the pragmatic parent, the business owner, the strategic thinker. My mother is a beautiful woman with great self-belief that likes to think big, hope and work at her ideas even when she has a 1% chance at accomplishment. And the surprising thing is, more often than not, she succeeds. As a teenager she was a finalist in the Miss India national beauty pageant, and last year in early 2013 she completed the Mumbai Marathon in just about 5 hours. Her friends told her that she was crazy attempting to run 26.2 miles for the first time, being in her mid-forties, but that didn't stop her from showing up at the beach at 6 a.m. every morning to train.

It was now time to reflect upon and sift out the advice that Ms. Francis and my parents had bestowed upon me. The one point that both my parents made in common was to aim high. I recollected an insightful quote by Nelson Mandela, ""There is no passion to be found playing small - in settling for a life that is less than the one you are capable of living." I spent that night browsing through different college admissions websites once again. It gave me an ounce of hope to read that most of them had no minimum score requirements and that applications were evaluated holistically. The websites were telling me to apply, my parents were, and so were my instincts. I logged into my Common Application account, sat in front of the College list page, and added every "dream school" I came across to my account.

Turns out that my mother was quite wrong! (As well-meaning mothers sometimes are) The additional applications did not simply cost me "a few hours" in time. They cost me a lot more than that. I had to carefully research each school, and put in much thought writing, drafting, re-drafting, editing and polishing my essays. However despite all the additional effort, a small voice inside me told me it would be worth it. In a moment of inspiration, I made up my mind that I wasn't going to let anyone dissuade or discourage me from pursuing my goals. I wouldn't be able to live with the regret of not applying so I decided to just go all out. I mustered up every ounce of passion I possessed to get through the numerous applications, the supplements and the opinions of people around me.

Feeling determined that you're going to accomplish a goal is unfortunately much easier thought than done. As I began working through application after application, the deadlines loomed large in front of me and I wished I had used my leisurely summer more productively – the creativity required for writing essays tends to play hide-n-seek when a deadline is round the corner. Moreover, some essay prompts and topics were quite a challenge. I mean, it tends to be difficult to remember and then recount in the most flawless language one's most inspiring moment, most challenging incident and most motivating song when one is fighting against time. Moreover, some essays required of the applicants, really threw me off gear. One for example was:

> "The short film, Powers of Ten, begins with an aerial shot of a couple picnicking in a Chicago park. The camera zooms out 10 meters. It then zooms out again, but the degree of the zoom has increased by a power of 10; the camera is not 100 meters away. It continues to 1,000 meters, then 10,000, and so on, traveling through the solar system, the galaxy and eventually to the edge of the known universe. Here the camera rests, allowing us to examine the vast nothingness of the universe,

a black void punctuated sparsely by galaxies so far away they appear as small stars. The narrator comments, "This emptiness is normal. The richness of our own neighborhood is the exception." Then the camera reverses its journey, zooming in to the picnic, and—in negative powers of 10—to the man's hand, the cells in his hand, the molecules of DNA within, their atoms, and then the nucleus both "so massive and so small" in the "vast inner space" of the atom.

Zoom in and out on a person, place, event or subject of interest. What becomes clear from far away that you can't see up close? What intricate structures appear when you move closer? How is the big view related to the small, the emptiness to the richness?"[1]

It took me about three attempts at reading the prompt before I could begin to interpret what it was asking, and even then I was extremely confused. "What in the world is this? Is this school crazy? How is anybody supposed to write these essays?" were thoughts that crossed my mind about a hundred times while I worked on my UChicago essay. Ironically enough, this school invites its students to suggest possible essay topics that go up on the application. Undoubtedly, these stretch the imagination and creativity of the applicants… and it made me feel like a school that values the intellect of its student body seems like a school worth attending. That thought encouraged me to pick my topic from the choice presented in the application form - I ended up choosing to "Tell the story of a street - real, imagined or metaphorical", which demanded every last drop of creativity and patience I possessed but once I was finished I shut the cover of my laptop with smug satisfaction, happy with the outcome of my essay. There is nothing better than the feeling of having one's potential and creativity challenged and then rising to the occasion.

It took me a few weeks to complete the rest of my applications, but once they were done I forgot about them and got back into the swing of school after the Christmas break. Then one, not very fine day in March 2009, the admissions decisions started coming in. I first heard back from Duke. Unfortunately they couldn't accept me. Apparently I was qualified and impressive but they had too many applications for the very limited seats. Then Brown and Cornell replied with the same story. I started getting a little alarmed at the number of thin envelopes that were coming in for me in the mail, with the typical rejection letter format, albeit worded diplomatically and sensitively which seemed to tell me – It's not you, honey, it's us. We wish we could accept more people because you seem great, but we can't because we're not large enough to accommodate everyone that wants us.

I started getting frustrated as more and more schools replied with regrets. I had a sinking feeling I would have to hear "I told you so..." from peers and authorities at school with whom I had discussed my college applications. My mother however continued to remain optimistic and provided that ray of hope during those dark, suspense-filled days. "It doesn't matter how many schools you don't get into, what matters is the ONE acceptance you need. And I'm confident that you're going to get into a wonderful school that is just right for you."

This time thankfully, she was right. A few days later, amidst the anxiety and stress of rejection, I received my UChicago acceptance. I was in the library at school, casually checking my email when it came:

Sender: University of Chicago Admissions
Subject line: Your Admissions Decision

My heart raced as I rapidly opened the email and clicked the link. My fingers shook as I typed in my login name and password, and the 10 seconds that it took to load the page felt like eternity. I'll never forget the moment I read the word, "Congratulations". I began screaming with delight and dancing in my school library, totally oblivious of the "Silence please" sign that is a prominent part of the Library décor. I couldn't believe what I saw in front of me. I read and re-read my acceptance - I had done it! I was going to attend a top-ranked school, a distinguished community of scholars. It didn't matter whether anyone thought I could or couldn't do it - the point is that it was happening. This was the first step towards actualizing my dream.

It would have been rather easy for me to listen to my counselor, put myself in the box of other "1900 SAT scorers" and apply to a school whose typical acceptance of median SAT score was closer to 1900. Breaking away from that, and realizing that there was a lot more to me than a number was probably one of the best mentalities I held onto through the college application process. And it got me where I wanted.

Eventually, my life would transform when I would fly twenty hours west of Ecole Mondiale World School in Mumbai across the Atlantic to Chi-city. This would not have been possible without a lot of work, perseverance, ignoring people who didn't believe in me, the support and encouragement of those who did, holding tight to my self-belief, cheering myself when in times of doubt and breaking some mental barriers in order to reach my destination.

Gradually, as the time to pack my bags and leave for Chicago began to draw close a fresh set of insecurities began worrying me. After overcoming the first hurdle of getting accepted, the bigger challenge now was sustaining, surviving and thriving through four academically rigorous years. I wondered whether I would fit in with the community of scholars. I wondered whether, despite my low SAT score I would manage to cope academically. I wondered whether I would find like-minded people and make fulfilling friendships. What would my life be like?

Perturbing thoughts continued to plague me the first time I stepped onto campus and took in the beauty that surrounded me. Was UChicago really the place as purported by students on chat forums as the place where "fun comes to die"? Where "squirrels are cuter than girls and more aggressive than the boys"? (I knew this one couldn't be true, I'm surely cuter than a squirrel!) Would I freeze to death during the six month long winter? I inhaled deeply and glanced around me. The crisp autumn air and breath-taking orange and purple leaves that adorned the trees seemed to tell me it would all be okay. Even if I failed, at least I would fail in a beautiful place.

College fortunately brought with it some pleasant realizations. For one, it shattered the image of the stereotypical UChicago kid, "the quirky nerd", as I realized that college is a place of vibrant diversity and it takes all kinds to make the world. I met some of the most amazing people with depth and warmth that made me feel at home, that served as family away from home. Social life rocked against the effervescent backdrop of Chicago with its stunning lakefront, busy downtown and neighborhoods. I ended up pursuing a range of interests, while also learning from some of the most interesting people I'd met. It challenged me intellectually, helped me grow academically while living in a world-class city. People with faith believe that whatever happens, happens for the best. In retrospect, it generally appears so. Today, after graduating, UChicago seems to be the most perfect school I could have attended.

The application essay writing process well foreshadowed my college experience. I was going to be pushing boundaries, I would be faced with some very challenging questions, and I would develop my philosophies and thought processes as I sought the answers. Most importantly, I learnt that pigeonholing oneself can be both dangerous and self-defeating because if one determines limitations before even attempting to pursue a vision, how will he or she ever be able to work wholeheartedly towards making it come true?

Before I progressed onto living out a fresh set of dreams those next four years, I took an important learning with me to college: **Never allow yourself to be limited by pre-defined categories**. Sometimes the categories are poorly defined, and mean girl or no mean girl, nobody should ever decide where you get to sit. We often underestimate ourselves without realizing that we are limitless beings with abundant potential. My SAT score didn't define where I deserved to be, nor did my academics through school or college. The strange thing is that categorizing is a natural process of life. From an early age, we tend to categorize ourselves and people around us. We have 'the cool kids' or 'uncool kids' in middle school, the 'athletes', 'losers', 'nerds', 'theatre geeks', 'out of our league' kids in high school; college is the perfect time to break those barriers and redefine oneself to build a new identity. Starting college is quite literally an opportunity to continue well-cultivated positive habits or turn over a new leaf in the book of one's life. You can be exactly who you want to – an opportunity to think and take decisions for yourself because you're suddenly less answerable to others and more to yourself. It is also a great time to experiment with diverse areas of interest, activities and pursue hobbies through the plethora of choices available on campus. The growth I experienced was a consequence of not limiting myself - I studied hard and was academically versatile, I opted for courses I normally wouldn't have dreamt of exposing myself to while at school; I also tried out a multitude of extracurricular activities. I lived abroad in Italy for a quarter, engaged in professional development and led an extremely fulfilling social life. I also didn't limit myself through the friends I chose: I socialized with the international kids, always had a bunch of people to say 'Hi' to every time I walked into a fraternity and occasionally studied with few academically and achievement-driven students who preferred to hang out mostly in the libraries too...just for inspiration when I began procrastinating school work. Ultimately one will gravitate towards the type of people one is best able to relate to, but it's important to meet all kinds of people in order to gain enrichment through exposure, in order to be able to sift out those that bring inspiration, joy and positivity to life. Make friends with people you never thought were 'your type': chances are you'll have the most stimulating discussions with those very people and learn a lot from them. There is an exceptional joy in engaging with people who are diverse, yet it is in that diversity that you tend to discover your own roots – it is a process of understanding the differences, celebrating the similarities and reinforcing what is uniquely your own.

The only constant in the world is change. Although most people have a tendency to settle down 'in a box' and repeat experiences, it is rewarding to embrace lifelong learning; always attempting to try and learn new things and maybe even master them. With its wealth of opportunities, college is the perfect place, the perfect time to start living out of the box and dare to sit at a different lunch table.

CHAPTER 3

My Affair with Chi-city: Food, Friends and Nights Out

"The city is not a concrete jungle, it is a human zoo."
- Desmond Morris

Life is a constant endeavour to adjust – be it to places, to people, to new situations. College, with all its merits, is a particularly demanding time for any teenager in terms of adjustment, but also a great time to develop the attitudinal framework and tools to be able to adapt to change – a skill that serves one well through life. You are away from home and family, (I must admit though, majority of young people don't view that as any kind of problem) you have to adjust to the climate and general norms of a new city and the busy campus environment. You have a new way of learning with elevated academic standards to adapt to, you are now exposed to a diversity of people that bring with them cultural, linguistic, ideological and intellectual diversity – from among these, you now have to make a totally new set of friends. It requires one to be able to respect the other with all the differences, while retaining one's roots and identity.

At times, students find it overwhelming. Some share their adjustment woes with others and get over it, some simply stay unhappy (not a great way to spend four potentially awesome years of your life), some seek a transfer and then there are the optimists who find ways to embrace the positives that come with the change.

Irrespective of the weather, the phase of college I was in, or my academic workload, I resolved that I would try to make the most of my professional and personal life. Staying happy was a conscious choice I made and being grateful for where I was helped me overcome the little daily adjustments I had to make. Investing time in getting to know my surroundings was the first step. I've learnt that every place is beautiful in its own way. Whether you're in a bustling city, suburban or rural setting, there will be aspects worth appreciating. Putting yourself in the frame of mind to positively take in what you're surrounded by, embracing it, savoring it and make it a part of your college experience can put you in a happy zone. You really begin to appreciate the wisdom in the words, "Life is how you see the glass - half empty or half full". Nothing is perfect so there is a reason some people love a place while others hate it - It all begins (and ends) with your perspective.

Like all places, Chicago has its pros and cons. Along with a world class city that has friendly people, rich diversity, a great food scene and vibrant nightlife comes the terribly cold weather that stretches on for months. One of my friends often joked saying, "Chicago has four seasons - almost winter, winter, still winter and construction." The university too has its share of perceived negatives. It is professed by many to be too nerdy, too academically intense and located in an unsafe neighborhood. Over the years, students have come up with self deprecating tongue-in-cheek slogans such as, "UChicago: Where fun comes to die", "Hell does freeze over", "If it were easy, it would be your mom" and my favorite one of all, "UChicago: Where the only thing that goes down on you is your GPA." These slogans were further popularized when they made their way onto t-shirts. That said, UChicago is certainly an academically challenging institution, otherwise it wouldn't have the high regard and stellar reputation that it does among academic circles not to mention its numerous Nobel Prize winners. I found that the key to overcoming day-to-day challenges is twofold:

- Navigating through and processing what is most bothersome
- Consciously placing focus on the positives that the place has to offer

One of the bothersome aspects was the safety angle. Some areas of Hyde Park are notorious and we were warned at orientation to stay away from designated neighborhoods as close as two blocks south of the university's bounds. As a measure of abundant caution, we were handed out "rape whistles" which were to be used to gather attention in a threatening situation. Being concerned about the safety of my neighborhood, I took measures to find the ways in which I could better secure myself. It was reassuring to know that the university police, the UCPD, had an umbrella service for students who wanted to walk home safely. There was also a SafeRide program and nighttime shuttle service, although this resource was occasionally misused and jokingly referred to as the "drunk van" among students. In any case, the university's resources coupled with some commonsense measures to stay safe, like not walking around alone at night helped us navigate through the issue.

With regard to UChicago's nerdy reputation, my friends and I attempted as best as we could to lead balanced lives. We had our share of quality (and quantity!) study time, and then rewarded ourselves with fun activities afterward. We made numerous inside jokes about how some people used their library lockers to store their pajamas or chose to attempt graduating with five majors! In retrospect, the jokes added so much character to our school and experience. I would never have been able to enjoy the self-deprecating humor of UChicago if I didn't laugh and take it for what it was: light hearted humor.

The second step to attaining a level of contentment is by focusing on the best that the city has to offer. This is subjective and as every individual is unique, it is important to engage with what entices you, given that any city will have an array of attractions. Over the years I discovered new and wonderful things that are exclusive to Chicago. Set against the backdrop of the gorgeous Lake Michigan lies a pulsating yet laid back city composed of a diversity of individuals and communities. There are several cultural neighborhoods: Chinatown, Greektown, Devon, Little Italy and numerous civic amenities. Millennium Park hosts an ice skating rink in the winters and outdoor festivals and concerts in the summer. The UChicago Arts Pass also enabled students to visit various museums and art galleries within the city at discounted prices or sometimes for free. As I became more familiar with the city, I set my social life up in a way that allowed me to engage with its fun and finer aspects. When my friends and I outgrew parties at fraternity houses, nights out during my junior and senior years (as each one of my friends slowly turned twenty-one) transformed to throwing our hands up and grooving at one of the reputed and lively downtown nightclubs such as Cuvee. My fun-loving group of female friends that included Meher, Emily, Leela, Nicole, Amanda, Adriana and Sol, would frequently organize a lively night out at 'The Roof', our favorite rooftop bar overlooking the prettiest of the city's architecture and lights. Although alcohol holds no fascination for me, I thoroughly enjoy a great atmosphere, lively music, dancing and socializing. My sophomore year friends' circle from the dorm, Manos, Tiffany, Peter, Catarina, Sibei, Muhammad and Munir made Wednesday nights at McFaddens, a popular bar frequented by college students, a tradition. We spent almost every Wednesday night of our lives for a year at that bar. As we grew academically, our choice of hangouts and venues for socializing also evolved. McFaddens is admittedly not as classy as the nightclubs that became our choice as Juniors or Seniors, but we still had a fun time and to this day cherish the place for the awesome memories it provided us with.

Dinner out rarely meant McDonalds or any other generic fast food restaurant: Chicago has so much to offer a passionate foodie. Over the years I tried out the various cultural neighborhoods and Chicago's famous deep-dish pizza. When I felt over-indulgent, I occasionally treated myself to molecular gastronomy as Chicago is renowned for attracting some of the USA's most creative chefs and a line of restaurant choices at the up and coming Fulton Market. Apart from indulging in fine-dining cuisine, I enjoyed creating my very own and personal fun little traditions within the city. Catarina and I both adore chocolate, and once a month we would make a trip downtown to the Godiva store and use our rewards cards to sample free chocolate. We would then cross the street and go over to the Hershey factory, grab some free samples and finish off our trip at the Ghirardelli store right across from Hersheys that also doled out a free chocolate square to everyone who walked in. Yes, we loved our chocolate and it somehow tasted so much better when free! (On this note, I must share that 'Free Food' becomes a great way to lure young people to various student organization events. For those of you in leadership positions in event planning - this strategy usually works in garnering a large crowd)

As if that wasn't enough sugar, we decided that every Wednesday we would snack at the C-shop, one of our favourite hangouts on campus. It was traditional for the C-shop to sell milkshakes for $1 on Wednesdays and the lines for these shakes sometimes got a little crazy, and understandably so. You're probably thinking of us as cheap girls who love sugary foods. Well, you're right about one of those two assertions. The truth is, we'd save our pennies to splurge on exquisite deserts at fancy downtown restaurants on days of the week that weren't Wednesdays.

Life was full of fancy events, frequent dinners, Michigan Avenue shopping sprees and clubbing but also had many small and simple pleasures that brought immense joy that we looked forward to. The C-shop milkshakes, hanging out at cafe's, sitting on the steps of

Hutchinson Courtyard completing afternoon reading, relaxing in the grass on a nice day out. Creating good times with close friends was key in keeping me happy. Itir, who was my roommate during my senior year, and I both love to cook. We'd often whip up delights, and host parties for our friends. Itir was an amazing hostess, and enjoyed having intimate get-togethers at our home. Luckily we lived in a large apartment complex where most of our friends were a few doors down. Itir also had a tea tradition: every evening, her best friend Alara would come over and they would use Itir's beautiful tea stash (she always had a stock of incredibly fancy teas from around the world) and together they would sit by the pot and chat as they poured cup after cup in her Turkish glasses. Alara, who later grew to become my close friend too would often say, "Honestly Neha, it is my evenings with you and Itir that are saving my sanity. They're the perfect study breaks from my thesis, which is taking the life out of me." Alara was a driven girl, who graduated a year early and headed straight to Cambridge University for a Masters program. Being the ambitious girl that she was, she certainly overworked herself in college, and her little tradition with a close friend made her time in college a lot less taxing.

Emotional well-being is the bedrock of an individual's ability to live, achieve, contribute and grow. Making time to unwind and relax with friends is vital; when times get tough and especially as one has been uprooted from family, friends serve as family and can provide tremendous personal support. This is the age to make close friends for life.

I also discovered that hosting parties is a great way to be socially active and enjoy time at college. Although it takes effort, it is a wonderful way to cement friendships, meet new people and keep life interesting. I moved out of the dorm in my Junior year, into a 32nd floor apartment of Regents, a high-rise by the picturesque Lakeshore Drive near downtown Chicago. Two of my building-mates, Faisal and Abdulla, an adorable pair of twins from Bahrain enjoyed hosting parties frequently at the open space on the top floor of our high-rise apartment building. Their sincere passion to give friends a good time, watching them entertain with patience and care for detail and simply revel at having people over taught me the value of being a good host – and how special a guest can be made to feel. I will always cherish the grand Great Gastby themed bash they organized, where everybody came donned in their fanciest attire. Abdulla, who also mixes music in his spare time, played DJ accompanying the fancy masks and beverages with great music. We had a gala time. Even when our dear friend Harsh's birthday rolled around, the twins put together a wonderful surprise party. Harsh walked into their apartment expecting to see only a few friends, but was surprised instead with a massive cake, a larger spread of food and about a hundred of his friends yelling "Surprise!" which we later followed by a night out at Cuvee, our favorite club. Not only did the occasion warm Harsh's heart, but the anticipation added surprise, suspense and excitement to our week. To date, Harsh and our friends relive this night with fondness.

As special events added spice to the mundaneness of our lives, so did the seasons. Chicago has a notorious reputation for its weather - and I discovered that one cannot truly estimate the hardship of a long, cold and windy winter unless one has experienced it first hand. Winters in Chicago aren't known to be friendly, especially to people like myself that have lived in tropical countries their whole lives. In Mumbai, I was accustomed to hot summers and warm winters, year after year, with unfailing reliability. Walking across the University's famed quadrangle, popularly known as the quad, trying to make it to class bundled up in 4 layers and still having my teeth chatter as a strong blast of wind would blow my way wasn't a pleasant adjustment to make. My first year was a little challenging in terms of accepting the climate, but I learnt that in order to be happy I'd have to look at the bright side. (Even though, quite literally, there wasn't a bright side. The sun shone very conservatively, if at all, on some days.) I resolved that I would make the most out of the situation and again, embrace the positives that came with seasonality. Ice-skating with friends at Millennium Park and snowball fights became a routine highlight of winter quarter. Catarina and I would make our way to Christmas markets and be fascinated by the falling snowflakes that surrounded us amidst the decorations. We began to appreciate the simple pleasures in life, like a warm cup of hot chocolate by a blazing fireplace. Looking forward to special activities made winters seem shorter than they were, and believe me, they were very, very long.

My mother often recollects my thread of emails to her. The December emails would typically rave about the beautiful white bed of snow, the gorgeous snowflakes, the bare trees holding the promise of spring and the breathtakingly pristine beauty that greeted me when I looked out of my dorm window. Emails in January would talk about, at length, all the fun activities I engaged in like ice-skating and snowball fights. By February I would start getting a little weary and would state how it was beginning to get a little bit much. The March and April emails would typically whine that it was high time that it stopped snowing and how I longed to swap my gloves, mufflers and boots for flip flops, sunglasses and shorts, and my desperation would be evident in the May email which would read, "Hey Mom, it must be warm and sunny back in Mumbai. Could you PLEASE export a little sunshine here to me? It's May and it is STILL raining and snowing." Because it seems like the winter never ends, Chicagoans tend to rejoice big-time when it finally does. Spring brings on happiness and sunshine. People walk the streets in their shortest shorts and remain outdoors as much as possible. In a strange way, winter days inspire people to make the most of long-awaited good weather when it does finally arrive and this stretches into the summer as well. I recall plenty of outdoor festivals and lazy days at the North Avenue beach during June and July. People and campus organizations have a host of barbecues as good weather becomes yet another thing to be grateful for.

Learning to see the good in people, places and situations and simply being happy is not too difficult, if one is appreciative. It is said, "Gratitude is the best form of prayer". Something as humdrum as the weather, or enjoying little pleasures of everyday life can add up to create feelings of positivity and joy. This becomes an asset to pull one through the temporary times when things get tough or rough. As Rhonda Byrne discusses in her book, *The Secret*, an optimistic frame of mind coupled with gratitude can truly change the way one perceives life and learns how to adapt.

CHAPTER 4
A 'Major' Problem

*"Your work is to discover your work and then
with all your heart to give yourself to it"*
- Buddha

Academics, academics, academics. They lie at the core of every college education, it is why (most) people are there. A typically diligent student will spend a great deal of time going to classes, discussion sections, problem set meetings and spending afternoons, evenings and late nights at the library, with multiple mugs of black coffee for company particularly before an exam or paper is due. Getting into the rhythm and navigating through the academic rigor can take a while. I certainly faced my share of academic challenges when I first began at Chicago. Coming from India, where the schooling environment is different, I had to undergo my gestation period before I became fully comfortable with the American system of education. Let me narrate an anecdote.

A boy who was used to getting straight A's in high school got his first college paper back with a "B-" on it in a bold red marker. He turns to the student next to him, a Chinese guy and asks what he got. "I got a B- too," he said. The boy sighed in relief at the knowledge that he wasn't the only student in class to not receive a good grade. "I'm not too disappointed though," said the Chinese guy, "this was the first paper I wrote in English."

Different people take different amounts of time to adjust to the change in academic standards. Some straight-A high school students have to get used to seeing B's on their transcript as the pool is suddenly more competitive and because the bar has been raised by a few levels. This is a normal and common phenomenon, and if you're one of the these kids, please don't worry; that odd 'C' on your freshman year transcript most likely won't be the factor that determines whether or not you succeed in life. You can also inquire about additional resources such as a college sponsored tutor program where you can sit with a tutor, library research materials or even the teaching assistant in your class. They are there to help and most colleges are rich in resources to aid and augment academic success.

My greatest struggle at the College though, didn't have to do with adjusting to the increased demands on my time and mental faculties or optimizing resources. When I entered the portals of UChicago as a freshman, I fell into the "confused bracket" that is, the set of kids who had no idea what they wanted to major in. While many of my friends knew that they wanted to be Econ majors or Premeds from the get go,

I was wondering and wandering. I vaguely knew that my interests lay in Economics. As the University of Chicago is world renowned for the strength of its Economics department, I thought that I may as well major in that subject. Prior to entering college, I had always heard of the importance of doing what you love, but I could never truly relate to the sentiment because I hadn't been able to pin-point to exactly what it is that I "loved". I liked numerous subject areas - languages, cultures, economic policy, but wasn't absolutely passionate about any one. Plus, being an ambitious person who desires to be self-sufficient, I knew that I had to monetize my interests in the real world. I had to make money once I graduated, lots of it preferably. Since Economics majors generally tend to do well for themselves career-wise, I decided to follow the herd and become an Econ kid.

Every grain of logic told me that I had made a great decision. UChicago is ranked right up there for its Economics program, brimming with award winning faculty delivering a rigorous academic curriculum. Twenty-five Nobel Laureates in the field have been affiliated with Chicago; as recently as November 2013 two of its faculty in Economics, Eugene Fama and Lars Peter Hansen were awarded the Nobel Prize for their analysis of asset prices. Contributions in the field are so illustrious that an entire school of thought, viz. the Chicago School of Economics, is associated with the University's name. I was excited to be taking a class from renowned faculty such as Professor Steven Levitt, the author of Freakonomics and Superfreakonomics. During my freshman year I had the opportunity to attend a talk by Professor Raghuram Rajan, another phenomenally inspiring UChicago faculty member. Dr. Rajan is believed to have caught signs and predicted the global economic meltdown as early as 2004, discussed in further detail in his book 'Fault Lines: How Hidden Fractures Still Threaten the World Economy' published in 2010. He was the Chief Economist at the International Monetary Fund from 2003 to 2007 and is currently the Governor of the Reserve Bank of India. Being in the presence of such renowned personalities in the field, I grew to be determined to leave UChicago with an Economics degree under my belt. It seemed to be 'the perfect match' for me.

My affair with the subject had begun in high school itself. I had flirted with Economics by opting to take it as a Higher Level subject for the International Baccalaureate. Learning about its various facets from microeconomics to international trade and development engaged me enough to want to take my relationship to the next level in college. I was ready to become serious, commit and plunge into the major with all those award-winning members of faculty to guide me intellectually.

Most schools in the United States allow students to take classes in a variety of subject areas and I was grateful for this opportunity to explore. Before beginning coursework related to one's major, the University of Chicago, like many reputed institutions of learning, wisely requires undergraduates to pursue a broad education to ensure that its students graduate as well- rounded, informed citizens. Only a third of courses taken typically fall within the major. The other two-thirds are distributed between a common core curriculum and electives, which are classes that can be taken in any field of study. This allows undecided majors to experiment with courses before they declare a major, and lets decisive students possibly double major or minor in a different field, or simply take a multitude of classes they fancy. The core curriculum was designed with the aim of helping students develop critical thinking and analytical skills across a variety of disciplines, whereas the major is to ground them with an in-depth understanding of a specific field. I loved the idea of benefitting from both a core and electives, and this broad based educational philosophy is what drew me to colleges offering this approach in the USA - Harvard, UChicago, Columbia to name a few.

As anticipated, my experience with the core curriculum was fantastic. As a first year student, I started out with the required courses in the humanities. I chose to learn about Media Aesthetics, and when I signed up for this class it sounded intriguing, but I honestly had no idea what that even meant! The sequence was titled "Media Aesthetics: Image, Text, Sound", and I thought we would look at some pictures and listen to a few songs, maybe read a book or two. It sounded interesting and perhaps, in my uninformed opinion, less tedious than the other humanities classes, 'Readings in World Literature' and 'Greek Thought and Literature', and less obscure than the one titled 'Human Being and Citizen' and 'Philosophical Perspectives in the Humanities'. I went in with an open mind expecting a few surprises. Luckily, all surprises that came my way were pleasant as I was assigned to a professor that was extremely passionate about his work.

The Media Aesthetics class was taken by a very aesthetic gentleman - Dr. Neil Verma, who was an attractive half-Indian half-Canadian man that had the most perfectly slicked - back hair. He was a zealous professor who wrote papers and blog posts examining the influences of culture on media, and was able to deliver each segment of the Media Aesthetics course with interesting examples and challenging questions. Despite being faced with a classroom full of confused freshman that didn't really know what to expect, it only took him a few weeks to pull insightful discussion and high levels of engagement from the class. It was very easy to see that he was enthusiastic about the subject, and this ended up being contagious. At the end of the term, one of my peers wrote on his evaluation, "I would describe him as Socrates' vision of a philosopher in the Theatetus." (You can see why UChicago kids tend to have a reputation as nerds...) Another said, "Dr. Verma is fabulous at leading discussion. He knows what he is talking about, is passionate about the course and topic, and knows how to motivate independent thinking. I thoroughly enjoyed writing papers for this class as most of the prompts allowed for creative thinking mixed with substantive, intellectual writing. He brought out my creative best, inspired me to think in a number of ways and changed my thought process." It was relatively easy for this enthusiastic professor to bring out the best from his class.

Personally, this course had such an impact on me, that at the end of my freshman year I ended up doing something quite out of character – at least quite a departure from the person that I was prior to entering college – I ended up detouring to Spain on my way home to India for the summer. I visited the Prado museum in Madrid to admire Spanish artist Diego Velazquez's painting *Las Meninas* that we had spent much of the year discussing in Media Aesthetics. And that trip was well worth it! Now this move, as I mentioned, was quite a departure from the Neha that my family knew me as. Let me explain...

It wasn't that I hadn't been exposed to art before. I am the eldest of three siblings and my growing years were fun-filled in the lively company of my younger sister Mehek and brother Armaan. We are evenly spread out with an age gap of three years between each of us. Growing up in a home with three children was "at times crazy but mostly fun", as my mother would aptly describe those years. My parents, in their earnest attempt to introduce my siblings and I to art, music and all the finer things in life, ensured that visits to some of the most renowned museums in the world were part of our family summer vacation itineraries. Hence I ended up visiting the Louvre in Paris, the Uffizi in Florence and the like. As a child, I would strongly resist such efforts as I found that museum visits were boring and preferred to spend vacation time at an amusement park, at the theatre or at a restaurant. I simply could not fathom how folks could spend long hours contemplating the Mona Lisa or gape in uninterrupted fascination at Michelangelo's David when roller coasters and culinary delights were beckoning.

So, after freshman year, when I declared my desire to visit Madrid especially to make a trip to the Prado, my mother was incredulous! She couldn't believe I was the same daughter who, a couple of years before, had opted to sit outside the Uffizi gallery in Florence to relish a gelato while the family took their time to admire the artworks within. Her skeptical reaction to the announcement of my idea of a good summer, still rings in my ears: "Honey, are you feeling okay? Did you just say that you want to go to Madrid especially to visit a museum? I can't believe it!"

I had changed – my tastes had evolved to cultivate an appreciation for art, and this was thanks to excellent, spirited faculty like Dr. Verma. Being taught by someone knowledgeable, energetic and passionate about the subject, made me want to care more about learning.

One of the first observable life lessons I absorbed from the University of Chicago was the importance of passion. After my pleasant experience in Dr. Verma's classes, I learned to scan course evaluations for engaging professors prior to signing up for classes. I was fortunate to have the exposure to many intelligent professors that were experts in their field, and thoroughly enjoyed what they taught. A second class that I will always remember with a faculty member that was in a field that he loved was a theatre course I took to fulfill the fine arts core requirement. Professor David New was a play director in Chicago who taught a few drama classes. It was obvious that he cared deeply about his subject: he went beyond what was required, encouraged students to watch plays in the city and discuss the impact of the production. "I don't want your responses to be academic analyses of the themes, actors or set. I know you all are very smart. I want you to tell me how you feel. How did the play affect your emotional state of being?"

It has often been debated as to what is a more critical ingredient for success – is it passion or is it focus? Watching Professor New teach with both - passion and focus on personal response, made me reflect on and realize the importance of feelings and feeling fulfilled through the working process. Everything we pursue in life, whether it's a job or a relationship is with the ultimate aim of providing positive feelings of happiness and fulfillment. Even if one's goal might be to make a lot of money, the money is eventually a means to an end – a means to purchase goods, services and comforts that bring satisfaction. Accomplishing something worthy is great, but working passionately and feeling fulfilled along the way can be a game changer. As is true for most things in life, the journey towards a goal counts.

Inferring life lessons by watching other people is of course, easier observed than practiced. While I saw the importance of being passionate about one's work, I found it rather difficult to implement when it came to my own life.

It was early on in my second year in college; I was well into the core and I had started taking the required courses for the Economics major. I charted out a plan of action with my academic advisor prior to starting the year, and began following it to the T. The first few weeks of a new quarter are always thrilling, and I began my Economics major courses, 'The Elements of Economic Analysis and Multivariable Calculus' with much enthusiasm. When week four hit, my excitement started dwindling. The pressure of problem sets and midterms intensified, and I found myself struggling in the economics class.

I'm not typically one to run away from challenges. I like to confront them head on, and having been in university for a year I knew well that classes tended to get demanding after the initial few days. My struggles with economics however were different. I would receive a problem set, sit down to crack it, and find myself mind-boggled in pages and pages of calculus. Even after spending numerous nights in the library working through my assignments, at the end of it I would ask myself the one question every college student at some point, maybe at several points, asks themselves, "How is this going to help me in my life?"

I asked myself that question at least a hundred times that quarter. I not only found what I was doing irrelevant to what I saw myself doing professionally but also uninteresting. Although I still was not sure what exactly I wanted to pursue as a career, it simply did not feel like my purpose in life was to wake up each morning and solve Lagrangean equations and derive Marshallian demand functions. The subject did not click with me - the deeper I got into it, the more I began disliking it. The thought of continuing this way for the next three years was most unwelcoming – in fact, it petrified the living daylights out of me.

At this point, assuming that I would decide to drop Econ, another dilemma presented itself - I had no clue what I would major in instead. I gave my biggest advocate and supporter a call. "Mom," I said seriously, "this class is driving me insane. The problem sets are difficult to get through, I'm so scared about the midterm and I just don't think I'm good at this subject." My mother patiently heard me out and asked how I was doing in the class. Upon hearing that I was slightly above the average, she said, "You're obviously better at this than you're giving yourself credit for. Stick it out a little. Let the midterm pass before deciding that you're really so bad. Everyone has rough patches, and you've hit yours. It'll pass - tough times don't last, tough people do." That was it. I had to be tough.

The midterm exam was the following week. Now I've taken a lot of exams in my school: middle and high school term exams, the IGCSE, the SAT (multiple times, fervently hoping that each successive attempt would yield a more 'acceptable' score than the prior one), the SAT subject tests, the ACT and the IB Diploma. Still, I don't remember being as scared for an exam as I was for that particular economics midterm. I began studying two weeks in advance (which, for most college students is akin to studying a century in advance given that our quarter system means that the gap between midterm and final exams is barely a couple of weeks), went through every single question on the problem sets about ten times. I borrowed Catarina's problem sets and went through those as well. I spent many nights in the library chugging highly caffeinated espresso drinks before trudging back to my dorm room at 5 a.m. I had done everything humanly possible to prepare myself. I was ready to rock this.

I went into the exam with mixed feelings of confidence and nervousness – confidence for having prepared really well but nervous because I wasn't sure how complex or difficult the questions would turn out to be. I was expecting a lot of long, confusing problems with complicated math. I was right about that one. It wasn't the best exam, even though I had prepared hard for it. I spent 90% of my time muddling around deriving equations. When the exam finally finished, I sighed with relief, skipped my next class, went straight to my dorm room and just slept. I was both mentally and physically exhausted, and didn't want to think about the torture that I had just undergone in the last hour and a half.

The following week I received the result of my exam. I had performed averagely well. Needless to say, I was unhappy with my performance – we UChicago kids generally tend to be dissatisfied with any letter that isn't an A. In my case, given the amount of effort I had put into studying for this exam, I felt like I deserved to have done much better.

For the next few weeks I thought long and hard about my decision to major in economics. It was a math intensive major, and math had historically never been my strong subject. It didn't come naturally to me, nor did I enjoy learning it. I enjoyed learning and evaluating the implications of economic decisions in the world, not the confusing math that went into theoretical formulation. I had to slog long hours in my classes and work extremely hard only to come out average. And the worst part of it was that I didn't see myself ever using any of what I was being taught.

Through this process, I kept talking to my mother. She felt that I should stick with what I pursued, and saw no reason for me to 'quit'. She played the devil's advocate quite well and constantly reminded me of the pros of sticking with the major, "Neha, you'll have fantastic career prospects being an Economics major from UChicago. Be it investment banking or consulting, you'll have an easy in. Besides, you're not failing the class so I don't see why you're quitting. I know you've had to work hard, but grow up - you'll have to work hard no matter what you choose to do if you want to see success. Welcome to being an adult!"

I found myself at crossroads. The core issue was that if I chose to give up majoring in Economics I would be perceived as a failure, and I didn't want people, whether it was my family or friends to think that I had failed. Worse still, I feared that I would see myself as a failure in my own eyes. But I really didn't want to continue with the major either. I knew in my heart of hearts that even if I did kill myself finishing it, it just wasn't for me.

I had done a summer internship with a renowned global consulting company and my biggest learning was that consulting didn't excite me enough for me to make a career out of it. In situations like this, does one think rationally or with their heart? Does one follow reason or instinct? Would giving up the economics major put my future career prospects at risk? What would I major in instead?

Many questions raced through my mind and I eventually listened to my heart and based my decision on an inspirational quote that happens to be one of my father's favorites. *"It doesn't matter what you do, as long as you're the best at it."* Was I the best at Econ? No. Would I ever make the best investment banker or consultant? No. Would I ever be able to use what I was being taught to be the best at something? No. Was I behaving like a failure? And really, the answer to that question was also No. I could not put my heart into it, so I decided to take myself out of it. Luckily for me, the system afforded the flexibility to change my mind.

This is precisely one of the reasons I chose to study in the United States. Only a handful of other nations have college systems that allow undergraduates to switch and transition between disciplines as seamlessly as the USA. It affords students the opportunity to change their minds as they immerse themselves in the program. In my home country, India, there is a clear distinction between sciences, commerce and arts. Once students commit to a stream, they can only specialize within that stream. If they decide to change tracks, they must start over and will not be able to graduate within the stipulated time. What saddens me is that there is a judgement associated with each field - those that pick science are generally considered to be the brightest fish in the pond. Only those achieving a high percentage of marks in their examinations are considered for admission, without much regard for their extracurricular profile or writing and analytical skills. Commerce comes in next, with Arts being at the bottom of the rung. Unfortunately, students distinguish between the streams and there exists a slightly derogatory perception around the Arts field. I believe that the Indian education system, barring the pre-school and primary levels, will require some serious modifications in order to compete in our increasingly globalized world. Switching of careers is becoming more common and technological advancement is rapidly creating jobs, some of which we could not have fathomed a couple of years ago. The way in which one learns and the ability to carry on learning is growing to be more important than the knowledge itself. In my case I was fortunate enough to receive an international education and be afforded the flexibility of switching majors in college, which served me well. I not only switched majors, but also chose two specializations and decided to leave college with two degrees.

After I decided that I did not want to continue with Econ, I focused my energy not on asking people what I should do but rather explaining why I chose to transition. After all, I was the one that had to sit through the problem sets, midterms and finals, not my friends or family and only I knew best what I was and wasn't capable of doing. I refused to be my own worst enemy by putting myself through what felt uncomfortably stressful.

At this point, I still didn't know what alternate major I would select. It was all very nice to say to my friends, "Oh, I realized Economics just wasn't for me. I'm simply not passionate about it." The next question that usually followed was, "So then what is it that you are passionate about, dear?" I still had no clue what the answer to that question was. As course registration for the next quarter began, I decided to forget about my finding my life's calling right away and not worry too much about not having an answer. I also decided I was so fed up of solving math problems, all I wanted the next quarter was to write papers. I signed up for a class called "Contemporary Global Issues", which did have a small economics component, but it was more about the international implications of trade and other policy implementation rather than derivation of formulae. I was just looking for a class where I could use my natural strengths like analysis and expressive writing to excel, and I ended up thoroughly enjoying the course. One step led to the other, I continued taking what I felt I would be best at with passionate faculty members and eventually I developed a strong liking for the study of international issues.

As I continued taking courses, I fine tuned my interest to the study of international policy, and ended up double majoring in International Studies and Public Policy Studies. Towards the end of my second year, I took a class on the plethora of cultural, economic and political issues in my hometown Mumbai. I was so intrigued learning about problems I didn't even know existed, that I ended up writing my bachelors thesis comparing slum redevelopment policy implementation in Mumbai and Rio de Janeiro. My wonderful professor, Ms. Tarini Bedi led me through this process and was willing to work with me despite the fact that I attempted to do it a year ahead of schedule, because she saw that I cared about delving further into the issue. She was one of my most influential college mentors, a strong and beautiful woman whose words will always stay with me. "As an academic, I promise you I don't make that much money. But it's alright because I wake up everyday excited by what my day will be filled with. I love traveling, writing and teaching and my profession allows me do all of those together. So I'm happy."

While my thesis writing process was underway, I still took some economics courses, those that were focused on policy implications with the kind of thing I liked engaging in. One class I will always remember fondly is the Economics of Crime, which is an Economics and Public Policy course. I was fortunate enough to have the opportunity to be taught by Professor Steven Levitt, who is renowned for his work in the field of crime. As I expected, he turned out to be another extremely passionate faculty member and one of the most practical people I have met. Once during the course he even said that chances are nobody in the real world would ever ask the Econ majors to solve a Lagrangean, which made me like Levitt a little bit more than I already did.

I also gradually developed a love for the International Studies major, and everything that came along with it. A mental picture of what I saw myself succeeding at and enjoyed began taking shape. I organically tended to make friends with other international students - I love listening to my roommate Itir speak in Turkish and friend Catarina from Rio de Janeiro feed me Brigadeiro, an absolutely delicious Brazilian chocolaty delight made with cocoa powder and condensed milk. I like talking to my friend Tiffany and comparing the differences between the lives of an international in Mumbai versus Beijing. I began to appreciate cultural differences and developed a deeper understanding of diversity both in an academic setting and through informal interaction that my vibrant campus, with students from various nationalities, ethnicities, sexualities, gender identities and economic statuses, allowed for.

During the fall of my senior year, while my contemporaries in Chicago were enjoying the cold weather, I went abroad and studied Roman civilization and Italian language for three months in Rome as a requirement for my International Studies major. Whether through classes, friends, for my thesis or study abroad experience, I was engaged in my work and enjoying how my courses were gradually transforming me into a global thinker and culture connoisseur. It seemed like I had found my calling, and I discovered it by taking the bold decision of breaking out of the cookie-cutter mould, and then taking baby steps and embracing areas of interest as they came along.

When one is doing what one loves, success tends to come more naturally and with relative ease. As a result of enjoying my work, I managed to find the time to pick up a second major in Public Policy Studies and finish my coursework for both degrees two quarters ahead of my class. I was also awarded special honors, because the work I put in towards my thesis didn't feel like "hard" work, yet it was work of good academic standard. Additionally, I received the wonderful opportunity to lead a team of researchers that evaluated the standards for green certification of restaurants in Chicago as part of one of my classes for Public Policy. We worked with restaurants and conducted cost-benefit analyses by examining practices in waste management, water usage, food and beverage, fixtures, etc. to see how restaurants could be more environmentally sustainable in a financially feasible way. Our research was extremely well received through a presentation and comprehensive report directed towards the Green Seal. It was a project that involved immersing ourselves in a local issue and creating a new policy towards resolving it. I was grateful to have received this phenomenal, hands-on learning opportunity.

I thought that the work for this class was over when the academic year ended. Dr. Sabina Shaikh, our professor mentioned that there would be a few unpaid internship opportunities for students interested in taking the research further and implementing it through a pilot program over the summer. Interns would work with the Green Chicago Restaurant Coalition in guiding target restaurants through the newly devised certification process. This sounded like an opportunity I would have loved to take up, but I had to be realistic and find a paid internship perhaps in the international division of a prominent global corporation. I went and spoke to Ms. Lee Price, the program administrator for the Public Policy department to give her general feedback on the class a few months prior to summer. She was extremely impressed to hear about our level of research and my involvement as a leader and asked why I didn't consider taking up the summer internship the professor had offered. I was honest in telling her that I wanted a paid position over the summer, as I wanted to earn some pocket money. I conveyed to her quite matter-of-factly, that while the prospect of seeing my research come to fruition was extremely attractive, what was stopping me from taking this up was the fact that it would be an unpaid internship. As luck would have it, she uttered the following golden words; "there is always funding available for somebody that is good enough and deserving of it. You need to have self-belief and an idea worth backing. Write me a proposal of exactly what you've done and what you'd like to continue doing, and I'll see what we can work out with the department." I ran home, submitted document on document about everything our team had done and created a proposal for how the summer internship would benefit me, the community, the department and every other potential stakeholder I could think of. Later that month Ms. Price got back to me saying that I had been awarded the Albert Svoboda grant of $2,000 through the Public Policy Studies department to spend a month working on implementing our research through the Green Chicago Restaurant Coalition. It was amazing, because that was more money than I would make on a monthly basis working a regular student internship. I was amazed at the manner in which doors were opening up for me - I just continued working hard at what I liked.

Monetary concerns, both during summer internships and after graduation are a serious issue for a majority of students I've encountered. My academic journey in college taught me the importance of being true to oneself and one's interests. I wasn't truly passionate about formulating economic theory or calculus, and this reflected in my attitude and approach towards the Economics major. I found it difficult to succeed despite working hard, and chances are I wouldn't have landed a job as an investment banker even if I slept fewer hours than others did preparing for interviews. On the other hand, following my interests resulted in a good measure of academic success, opened doors and above all made me feel worthwhile and fulfilled.

In Confucius's words, "Choose a job you love and you will never have to work a day in your life." I'd seen the value of professional passion through Dr. Verma and Professor New, and the contagious domino effect it had on my enthusiasm towards learning. I'm fortunate to have found my passion in college and I'm hoping that I will attain professional success in the world pursuing what I love. Like Professor Bedi, I want to wake up each day ready to jump out of bed and be charged about going to work. **Never compromise on what you love and "settle" for something that makes you unhappy.** What if you don't know what you love? What's the best way to find it? As Rumi says, "What you seek is seeking you." The secret in his saying lies in the fact that it starts with you. It is best to follow your heart and instincts rather than the herd, engage with what you seem to be attracted to, play on your areas of strength. People often deliberate on what is a greater ingredient for success: competence or interest. The two pieces of the puzzle that need to fit together are: enjoying what you're doing, and being good at it. Chances are if the former is in place, the latter will follow.

CHAPTER 5

Citius, Altius, Fortius: Faster, Higher, Stronger, and ....Fatter!

"Growth begins when we start to accept our own weakness."
- Jean Vanier

The Olympic Motto implies improvement and progression; an aspiration of excellence and being the best that one can be. College is a time when this aspiration is tested and challenged. Amongst all the highs and good stuff, some of the likely challenges students face include severe homesickness, adjustment issues, culture shock, academic and other pressures. Different students employ different coping mechanisms. College offers a plethora of platforms and opportunities - it is a time of exposure when you will be faced with lots of choices. The small choices that one makes in daily life slowly become habits. These habits shape us – they can make us or they can break us, so one has to be particularly careful to avoid falling into the trap of faulty habits and make a conscious effort to choose positive, life-reinforcing ones. Let me share how my freshman year went downhill in a way, due to my poor choices and what it took to pull up my socks.

Prior to leaving for the University of Chicago my best friend from high school Vandana, who anticipated attending Babson College that fall, had shared a joke with me: "When we get to college, we'll have to choose two of the following three: good grades, a social life and sleep." It took only a few months into my freshman year to realize that she wasn't kidding.

Juggling between enrolling in enjoyable classes, pursuing extracurricular activities and forming friendships, I spent much of my first year acclimatizing to changes and altering my lifestyle to create a perfect college experience. Balance was a priority: I didn't want to miss out on any one particular aspect of undergraduate life. I was infected with what is called "FOMO" these days, that is the Fear of Missing Out.

While I wasn't in classes, my afternoons were spent at the Regenstein library, a massive five-storey library that boasts of a collection of over 4.5 million print volumes. The Reg was the favourite hangout especially the night before exams, perceived as a Mecca for the academically driven, and a social haven for the others. My evenings were typically spent in meetings with the South Asian Students Association, Professors' office hours, at parties or having enlightening three hour long conversations at the dining hall. These were invariably very stimulating and lived up to the claim made by reputed American Universities that their intellectual communities provide opportunities to learn both in and out of the classroom. The fact that I had an unlimited meal plan and that I was "learning outside the classroom" often irrationally justified sitting in the dining hall for three hours engaging in those conversations. Needless to say, food or beverages almost always accompanied those food-for-thought discussions.

As Chicago is a world-class gastronomical hub, I explored new local restaurants and tried novel foods such as deep-dish pizza at multiple outlets. After all, I wanted to taste for myself whether Giordano's was truly better than Gino's, Eduardo's, Pizzeria Uno and all the other deep-dish places I'd heard of. Life was a beautiful breeze falling into its rhythm. Small ways of life took shape into habits, whether it was a few chocolate chip cookies after every dinner or University of Chicago's famed $1 milkshakes with my friends on Wednesdays. Mint chocolate chip and cookies and crème grew to be my favorites.

On the days that I didn't have time to sit for hours in the dining hall, a quick meal of fast food accompanied with french fries and a Coke sufficed. And of course, while on the go there was nothing quite like a bag of Peanut MnM's or a Hershey's bar. During midterms season when nights in the library became early mornings in the library, I would keep myself awake with sweet, ice-cream blended caffeinated beverages.

On weekends, my friends and I would enjoy frequenting nightclubs downtown, about 6 miles away from our campus. Being out until late, we wouldn't want to return home hungry. The obvious solution to this problem lay at a 24-hour diner or pancake house. I still remember the nights that I would wolf down 3 chocolate chip pancakes prior to returning back to bed.

American cafeteria dining was the biggest aspect of culture shock that I faced. Coming from India, food at home typically comprised of a wholesome meal of *dal, roti, sabzi* - lentils, homemade whole wheat bread and an array of vegetables often accompanied by a chicken or seafood gravy. My snack generally comprised of a plate of freshly cut fruit, or a glass of coconut water. Those were replaced by Oreos and doughnuts. High fat food, large portion sizes, fast food, candy and sweet drinks, late night eating and an unlimited meal plan in the dining hall were radical changes that took over my life. In the process of integrating into college life, unhealthy eating became a norm. Besides, I didn't have the time to focus on watching everything that I put into my mouth or procuring healthful and nutritive foods because I was busy juggling multiple pursuits.

I took pleasure in celebrating food-centered festivals such as Thanksgiving. The typically celebrated festivals in India, *Diwali* and *Holi* are centered around lights, fireworks and playing with color. *Ramadan*, which is observed by many in India, is in fact about abstaining from food and beverage through the day. So it was a refreshing change to be happily stuffing my face with stuffing and pumpkin pies on Thanksgiving. I reveled in the gradual changes in food choices, and being a positive person I attempted to enjoy the new ways of eating.

People often say that freshman in college gain about fifteen pounds - the notorious 'Freshman Fifteen' - and that a little bit of weight fluctuation is normal. Needless to say, the unlimited meal plan, $1 milkshakes caught up with me and while my new lifestyle was taking shape, I was steadily growing out of shape. I consoled myself saying that it was all right, I was fine and like most other students would lose the weight once I returned home. What I failed to acknowledge is just how rapidly I was piling on the pounds. By the end of my freshman year, I wasn't simply "fifteen pounds over". I had put on almost three times as much, making me a whopping forty pounds overweight.

Through my high school years, I had a tendency to be on the heavy side, but I had never been so big in all my life! As a result of gaining weight, many changes infiltrated my life. I went from struggling to pull up my jeans, to not being able to fit into them at all a few months later. I had to re-stock my wardrobe with looser sweaters and bigger pants. As I got larger, I began feeling breathless every time I'd climb a flight of stairs or walk a long distance. My concerned roommate spoke to me about my addiction to sweets and chocolates and suggested I start frequenting the gym. People around me began noticing the physical change in me, a few concerned souls inquired about how I was keeping and this began to have negative repercussions on me psychologically.

As the scale skyrocketed, I stopped stepping on it. It would just make me depressed. I began to be afraid to look into the mirror because I despised my chubby cheeks. My face had lost its shape, swollen out and as a result of unhealthy and rapid weight gain I had also acquired pimples and acne, which had never been part of my early teenage years. I began to lose confidence in myself because I had let myself fall into a trap. My exterior persona reflected a person who couldn't take care of herself, and this idea troubled me to no end. I neither looked nor felt very attractive, and this echoed itself in my behavior. As looks and confidence, self-image and sexuality are closely correlated, while my friends were going on dates, finding boyfriends, some were exploring their sexual side and hooking up, I never felt worthy or engaged in any of this because I felt I was too fat.

Being away from my family and a tad bit homesick, I sought emotional comfort in food. Chocolates were the best pick-me-up; I would buy a little cake or down a bar every time I felt bad about myself. Sugar had made its sweet spot in my bloodstream and whenever I was stressed due to academics or felt lonely and alone, I ate. Food had become far more than a fuel to provide life and serve vital functions. It provided me with emotional satiety. By the end of my freshman year, although I was a fantastic student on paper – making it to the Dean's List, enjoying a great social life with good friends, and being actively involved in the university community - I wasn't doing as fantastically well on the inside. My self-image had reached an all-time low. I began hiding myself behind oversized clothing and stopped attempting to look good or make an effort to dress well. I avoided being photographed or communicating through Skype. The way I spoke, thought and behaved had changed. I felt out of control and was starting to lose it.

In an attempt to reassure myself and get over my insecurities, I would often look around me at people larger than me. America has a good many oversized people and I would observe and scrutinize them in an attempt to feel better about myself. I began to compare myself to those more obese than me in order to console myself that indeed, "I wasn't that bad." I was in a weird, vicious cycle of feeling bad, eating, gaining weight, trying to break the cycle by making myself feel better only to binge on sweets again thinking that it was alright. I also came up with all kinds of lame excuses to keep eating. I mentally justified second dinners in February telling myself that people tend to eat more in the winter anyway.

By the time summer rolled around, I was relieved to be done with finals and on the plane back east. I was returning home to Mumbai, but stopped en route to join my family for a vacation in Spain. My flight landed in Barcelona early one morning in June, and I was looking forward to seeing my family after almost seven long months! The last time I had seen them was in December over winter break and I had changed significantly since then.

I hopped off the plane into sunny Spain and made my way to the W Barcelona, the beautiful beachfront hotel we were staying at. I was excitedly expecting a long round of hugs, kisses and "I've missed you's". As I walked up to the hotel porch my family was waiting outside to receive me. It took them a couple of seconds to recognize me, and once it registered they were simply flabbergasted.

My mother was the first one to react. "Hi my darling! Oh gosh, what happened? How did you gain so much weight?!" she asked as she hugged me tightly and ran her fingers down the pimples on the side of my face. She examined me closely, being the concerned and caring parent that she is. After a few seconds of scrutiny she attempted to cover up her shock with the excitement of seeing me but I could tell that she was mortified. My father held a more neutral reaction, welcomed me and smiled tightly as he took my luggage. My younger sister Mehek and brother Armaan weren't as diplomatic. "Dude, how did you get so fat?" Mehek inquired while Armaan twisted his lips into a silly looking, childish grin and nodded his head saying, "Not looking so good, NeNe. Looks like college isn't really suiting you."

Looking at my family so unpleasantly shocked by the person I had become sent an awful feeling to the pit of my stomach. I lowered my gaze as I felt sad, disappointed and angry at how I had let myself go this way and lost control. How did I allow myself to get so blinded? The magnitude of my condition hit me like a pile of bricks watching the people who cared for me most in the world. Amidst the exquisite Barceloneta beach and its attractive people, surrounded by an external setting that can only be described as perfect, I was sad and angry within. That was my defining moment. A fuse inside of me snapped as the anger got converted to determination. It was the first time that I mentally acknowledged that something had to be done – I needed to change my condition. I vowed to change my fate, and was going to take every step that I needed to.

Dealing with the fact that I had let myself go was bad enough, but that I had somehow let my family down only made it worse! After a few minutes, I looked at them smiled and said, "I know, I know, I've really let myself go. But give me a few months. By the end of this summer you will be looking at a different Neha. I know I need to eat better and exercise regularly and I will look into it as soon as we're back home. Now let's not mention anything about my weight or acne and enjoy this holiday, please! I promise you'll see a new person in a few months and you'll love me so much you won't want to send me back to college."

Everybody looked at each other and smiled as they heard something that reassured them - the desire to change, coming from me. Although I know that my family will love me unconditionally, it relieved them to hear that I was going to work at being healthier and better. My mother looked especially relieved - I could tell that she had already mentally planned out her well-intended nagging strategies, and lists of do's and don'ts - but seemed happy that she wouldn't actually have to employ them. We went into the hotel and spent the next two weeks enjoying our summer visiting attractions in Barcelona, Madrid, Cordoba, Granada and Marbella. Despite seeing beautiful monuments, museums, palaces and beaches, my mind was fixated on my weight. I would observe, in awe, the topless girls on Barceloneta beach not because I like to ogle at semi-nude people but because I was fascinated by the confidence and ease at which they displayed their bodies. I too desired that level of poise and the ability to be comfortable in my own skin.

I returned from my travels having reflected deeply, inspired to make the changes that I needed to. I knew that watching what I ate like a hawk or exercising daily wouldn't be easy, but I was driven by the mental image of a healthier me. That summer in Mumbai, the next thing I did after unpacking my bags was line up at Dr. Sarita Davare's clinic. Dr. Davare, a simple lady and insightful doctor, is a prominent dietician well-reputed for helping hundreds of patients shed thousands of pounds. She has a no-nonsense approach to weight loss and systematically guided me through a rigorous cleansing program that would flush out all the toxic junk I had put into my system. My green colored beverage went from being a mint chocolate chip milkshake to a cup of green tea. From enjoying heavy, gastronomically delightful meals out, I went to relishing home cooked, gastro-intestinally delightful vegetable based dishes. Fruit promptly replaced candy bars, my portions decreased to about half their earlier size and I concluded my last meal by 8 p.m.

Dr. Davare also instructed me to walk for an hour and a half each day. On my first day, I got through about fifteen of those minutes, huffed and puffed and decided to call it a day. My relatively sedentary lifestyle and hundred and ninety six-pound body didn't allow me to run or stretch as freely as I desired. I had to go for three walks a day in order to complete the target of one and a half hours but as I built momentum I kept going. A vision of a healthier me, and a constant reminder of my family's faces when they saw me in Barcelona pushed me to give it my all. I knew that if I didn't put in one hundred percent, I wasn't going to achieve results. As the saying goes, "All it takes is all you got." This (literally) was crunch time! Eventually, persistence enabled me to build up endurance. I went from barely being able to walk to running a few miles within a month. As I began taking care of my body, it began rewarding me in return. I started losing weight and the more that came off, the stronger and fitter I became.

Those three months, I lost about thirty pounds. When I returned back to Chicago to begin my second year, my friends were pleasantly surprised to see the new me. I definitely managed to make a few jaws drop, which made all the struggles, micro-controlling and sacrifices worth it. I no longer felt bad or wallowed in self pity about the days when I used to go out with friends and family to dine and watch their faces as they ate while I had to sit hungry because nothing on the menu fit into my diet plan. All the chocolates I'd given up didn't matter anymore. I was a new person ready to begin her new life.

Despite losing thirty pounds and changing my appearance, I revelled in my new self but also kept in mind that I was only halfway down the road. I still had to lose another thirty- five pounds in order to be at normal weight and fully happy with myself. Finding a way to integrate diet and fitness into my routine was a crucial step in sustaining weight loss. Through my second year, I made the time to visit the gym everyday no matter how late into the night. Although I was still on an unlimited meal plan, I limited what I ate and chose carefully rather than grabbing mindlessly. As part of the Biological Sciences requirement for the Core, I opted for a course in Nutritional Science in order to learn more about proper nutrition and making healthy lifestyle choices. The College also offered exercise classes, and I didn't hesitate to take the ones I fancied such as jogging and cardio kickboxing.

The habits I cultivated during this period have stayed with me. After moving off campus and off the meal plan, I continued to eat healthy by buying more fruits and vegetables when I grocery shopped rather than packaged, processed food. I found a way to balance my diet, indulge in the chocolates I love when I truly desired, but in moderation.

Exercise has now, become a part of my life- I practice yoga daily and in January 2014 I ran the Mumbai Half Marathon, a distance of about 13.1 miles. My mother, who is also an active runner, looks at me with admiration and often states that she cannot believe how her daughter has transformed. I too think back to the days when I could barely sustain a fifteen-minute walk and remind myself that I am never going back there.

It took a lot of work and patience to acknowledge my obese condition, make changes, progress, get comfortable in my skin and most importantly, accept and love myself. Through this process of transformation, I'm grateful to have formed healthy habits for life. Without making my health and myself a priority, I wouldn't have succeeded. I've come to realize that taking care of oneself isn't something that there will ever be time for - it is about making the time for what is important. Going back to the quote at the start of this chapter, I will add that accepting our own weaknesses, whatever they may be, is the first step towards transformation. **Having accepted the weakness, or identified the area for improvement, what follows are steps to improve and gradually small daily choices turn into lifelong habits that enable us to be the best version of ourselves.** And ultimately, most of you are likely to be responsible for nobody other than yourselves at this time in your lives. Take advantage of this and use it to build identity capital, identify your priorities and engage them with the best foot you can possibly put forward.

CHAPTER 6

Nothing Ventured, Nothing Gained

"Life begins at the end of your comfort zone"
- Neale Donald Walsch

We are creatures of habit who get accustomed to where we are and what we do. We often take things for granted, and tend to value comforts only when we can no longer enjoy them. Let me begin by giving a perspective of my comfort zone, what it entailed to transition from Mumbai to Chicago and how this change shaped me such that I readily embraced new vistas and adventures when they presented themselves.

My life in Mumbai was, by the average standard of a high schooler, just great! The value on education placed by my family gave me certain privileges such as a private international school education and a set of friends that came from some of the most influential business, political and Bollywood film industry backgrounds in Mumbai. Everybody loved living it up: there were social events almost every other day, clubbing on weekends, fancy meals out every week or so. Being a community - oriented culture, there were numerous opportunities to mingle and socialize be it at weddings or festivals. In Mumbai, the elite class that belongs to the upper end of the wealth spectrum comprises of people who all seem to know each other. Despite living in a populous city of over eighteen million people, I often felt like my world was very small: I knew everybody there was to know, and the inner circle was connected. There was also much domestic help. My laundry was done for me, meals were cooked fresh and served hot at lunch and dinner and a battery of maid servants were always around to make my bed, clean my room and bring me water when I was thirsty. I never had to deal with a dirty dish in my life or worry about grocery lists.

Needless to say, my maids, cooks and chauffeurs didn't quite follow me to college. I not only felt alone in the sense of not having my family and comfortable community around, but also didn't have help with my chores. Though this may sound rather trivial, it was quite an adjustment to be perfectly honest. I suddenly had to learn how to get my own water, procure my own groceries and make my bed if I wanted a clean room. Having an impeccably neat roommate my first year only added to the pressure on me to keep things in place. I learnt (the hard way) that one must always separate their whites and colors while washing clothes. At the end of my first three weeks in the dorms, I had to face the inevitable: laundry. Having never done it before in my life, I procrastinated this chore as long as possible. Alas, the day came when I ran out of undergarments and had to drag my hamper down into the basement of Max Palevsky Residential Commons. Being an amateur - a lazy amateur - I threw all my clothes in the machine at once. Despite having taken the time to read the instructions, reading the back of the detergent and scooping out the right amount of soap, I didn't know which buttons to push on the machine. My thinking at the time was, "hot water will kill all the germs." That experience ended with a mortified Neha whose white clothes came out tie-dyed pink.

Making these adjustments at first was complex. I won't lie - I sometimes missed my maids more than my parents. In an attempt to get through those chores, I would tell myself that this was the life that I had chosen and I now had to accept both - the pros and cons while attempting to stay focussed on the positives. Believing that everything I was doing would eventually benefit me also helped.

Repeat an action often enough and it becomes a habit - after a few months I actually began enjoying my chores! Once I got over the transitional discomfort it felt empowering to be able to take care of myself. I felt confident in my ability to live independently, and I concluded my first year in college knowing that if I ever had to survive without domestic help I could very easily do so. Fending for myself, which was such an alien idea at first became second nature to me that in fact when I returned home that summer it felt strange to ask people to bring me water. I'd get up and clear my own plates, and run my own laundry even though I didn't need to just because I had become so conditioned to being self-sufficient. Human beings are made to adjust, and when we manage to rise above discomfort we grow as individuals. Once this realization dawned, I became a lot more confident in my decisions centered on changing my fundamental lifestyle or taking risks beyond the familiar, whether it was moving into an apartment from the dorms or applying to study abroad.

Back at home my grandmother Daulat often says to her friends in Hindi, *"Neha ke pairon mein chakker lage hain"* literally translating to "Neha's got wheels on her feet." Now, I'm no pro-rollerblader, but like most people I too enjoy the idea of jet setting off to interesting, exotic locations and consequently take any opportunity I receive to travel the world. College presents a plethora of such opportunities to travel, be it spring breaks, summer internships out of one's college city, a chance to represent one's college as part of some team or the other, or study abroad programs. Experiential learning is the best kind of learning so I believe every undergraduate should learn through travel if possible. There is a bounty of new discoveries to be made and traveling truly helps one cultivate a sense of adaptability and confidence besides broadening one's social and cultural perspectives.

So, I moved and relocated thrice in the last five years. First of all was the move from Mumbai to Chicago. Then I spent a quarter studying in Rome and I will elaborate much more about that later in this chapter. Finally I enrolled in the 'Semester at Sea' program and spent four months living and learning afloat a ship and voyaged through sixteen countries post graduation. Needless to say that each of these experiences weren't easy to actualize. Going abroad isn't something you decide, snap your fingers and boom - you wake up on some beautiful beach or by a historic monument on the other side of the world the next day! There are many practical concerns, financial concerns in addition to painstaking planning that goes into fructifying a dream of spending time abroad with an educational purpose. Some of the questions that plagued my mind were whether I would manage to adjust to all the situations that presented themselves. How different would it be from my life at the moment? What is the worst thing I would have to go through abroad? And because I'm a rather social character who enjoys the company of friends, I always stressed out about whether I will make compatible friends and meet interesting locals who would add color to the adventure by showing me the city from the lens of a native. More than anything however, I wondered how the experiences would mould and change me.

I had to face the concerns of my family members too. For the longest time my parents debated whether sending me abroad for my undergraduate studies was a wise decision. They worried about how the culture would influence me and how safe the surroundings, particularly the notorious south side of Chicago, would be for a young eighteen year-old girl on her own. After I got through college unscathed, I assumed it would be alright for me to cruise. When I told my grandparents that after taking my college degrees, I planned on hopping on a ship for four months through the Semester at Sea program they thought that I was playing some kind of joke. Believing me came in second - for about a week they didn't even believe that a program like Semester at Sea existed. Upon showing them the website and my acceptance letter it dawned upon them that their granddaughter was indeed going to be globetrotting through sixteen countries around the Atlantic, and this led to a flurry of questions of how I expected my parents to allow a young, twenty-two year old girl to be off on her own. "Are the ports you're going to safe?" "Do you know anyone else on this voyage?" and "How is this going to help you in your life?" were a few of many, many questions I was faced to answer. Ultimately however I managed to confront them effectively enough to find myself on a flight heading towards the experience I desired. Each travel experience left an indelible mark on my mind, heart and personality as being out of my geographic comfort zone has had the greatest influence in transforming me through my college years. Although you may not feel like you need the transformation, deciding to place yourself in a foreign situation can broaden your horizons to the point of completely changing you. I will let the words of Augustine of Hippo make this point. "The world is a book and those who do not travel read only one page."

Studying abroad is a secondary affair: College itself is a platform to throw a person of any shape, size, color and way of life into the unfamiliar. It is a new environment for every incoming freshman and most young people making the transition have concerns about their ability to adjust. **Take advantage of this unfamiliar environment and all of the opportunities it presents to step out of your comfort zone. Challenge yourself by inviting change: the ability to adapt is a priceless trait in our increasingly globalized world.** Study abroad, if it is a financially viable prospect that fits into your academic schedule and if not benefit from the changed environment around you by getting out of your socio-cultural comfort zone.

I have learnt that being young gives one the courage to embrace challenges in various forms. This is because if you're able to work through them successfully, you'll have mastered new skills along with the wonderful feeling of accomplishment. If you lapse, you still walk away with the lessons. So use this time in your life to explore, take risks and discover your potential. That said, don't be intentionally silly and do anything that could potentially leave a permanent negative impact on your life, put your health or the lives and emotions of others at risk.

Now let me get to my Roman adventure. The core curriculum at the University of Chicago requires students to take up the study of a civilization. Numerous students choose to fulfill this requirement abroad as the College, besides offering the course on campus itself, has excellently designed programs in alternative exotic locations ranging from Paris and Barcelona to Pune and Beijing. I had considered studying abroad, but only began seriously looking into the prospect after switching my major to International Studies and realizing how much I had grown personally between high school and college. During the fall of my sophomore year, I began attending study abroad fairs, meeting the people who worked in the office and keeping my eyes open. As it needed to fit into my academic schedule, I began planning my quarter abroad in advance. Taking the time to understand the process is crucial as it can determine whether or not one gets accepted to the program of their choice. Planning ahead is also key, particularly financial planning, as many pieces need to fit together in order to enable studying abroad. I knew that I wanted to study somewhere in Europe and when I took the time to read through the brochures and website, I realized that the civilization studies program in Rome excited me most. The thought of living in a historically rich location with the most delectable cuisine drove me to piece together an application for the 'Antiquity to the Baroque' program. This wasn't a difficult task as I had taken the time to understand what the program offered, and I genuinely desired it. After being selected, I began gearing myself to move to Rome in the fall of 2012. I knew a few people going, but I wasn't particularly close to anyone. I got on the plane, left with my heart still in Chicago unprepared for what was about the come. I expected to travel quite a bit as I knew Italy was relatively close to Spain, Germany, France and many other European countries but most of my learning came from living in Rome itself, whether it was learning to navigate or adapt to people.

#college

    I landed in Rome, and during the drive from Fiumicino airport to the city I was taken in by the ancient splendor of the place. Having lived in Mumbai and Chicago I was used to the concrete skyscrapers of busy cities - this was busy but not quite in the same way. It was archaic in a glorious sort of way. The streets looked confusing, and every corner had a statue, some ruins or interesting set of steps. The beauty stunned me. Again, having lived in two bustling cities, I was accustomed to clubbing every now and then. I wondered where among these ruins lay the nightlife, if at all.

    I arrived at the villa where I had to pick up my keys and where some of the students in our group would be staying. I met everyone, said my hellos and enjoyed a pasta lunch with the group. As we were eating, in walked Nerjada with her three suitcases. As she lifted her Armani sunglasses I saw the beautifully made-up face of a luscious haired Albanian girl that spent much of her time growing up in New York. Nerjada (who insists we call her Ada) instantly became my favorite girl, and not just because she looks like an angel! Two minutes of conversation was all it took us to realize just how much we had in common: we were social people that loved sweets, fashion, our younger sisters and cruise vacations in the Bahamas. We were supposed to be roommates, and unlike everyone else in the program that had an even number of people in their apartment, we had a third person.

    Lauren Baumgartner arrived at the villa from rural New Jersey an hour after us. She came up the stairs manhandling her suitcase, and although she appeared to be angry, her face was drained of all color. Her hair was up in a messy ponytail and she was dressed in cargo type beige pants and a rugged tee shirt with a nondescript over-coat. How someone could wear that on an international flight was beyond my understanding. She stared at us. It didn't look like she had seen a ghost; she looked like the ghost.

    Ada being a sweetheart broke the ice and said, "Hey, you must be Lauren... I think we're roommates! Hi, my name is Nerjada, pronouced Ner-ya-da but no one ever calls me that... just call me Ada, its easier."

    "And I'm Neha," I chimed in.

"Cool" was her response in the most dull and flat tone I've ever heard. She hesitated a bit and a few seconds later said, "Uh, I'm sorry I don't travel very comfortably. I just woke up from being sedated, and besides, I'm not the most social person but it's nice to meet you guys."

Ada and I looked at each other. "Its okay," said Ada softly, "that flight was super long, I totally understand," although she didn't quite look like she understood.

Matt, a guy in the program who was talking to us before Lauren arrived was standing there looking amused at the clear distinction between our personalities. In an effort to instigate us he said, "You know, you are the only three to have an odd number of people in your apartment. What if there are two rooms and one of you gets a single? How are you going to decide who rooms with who and who stays alone?"

Ada and I instinctively looked at each other, pointed at each other and said in unison, "We can be roommates." I only realized how terrible that must have looked after it came out. I felt a little bad for making my negative first impressions of Lauren so obvious to everyone around me. Despite my best intentions to be friendly, strike a chord and be nonjudgmental of all the new friends I was about to make, I couldn't help what had just happened and I felt a twinge of guilt. I think Ada also realized as she covered up by saying, "Of course we can do it either way...I really don't care." Matt, at this point, was extremely amused and as Lauren went away to get her keys he gave us a smirk and said, "Have fun, you two."

We gathered our belongings and left to catch a cab to Trastevere, the neighborhood where our apartment was located. On the way we chatted with Lauren a little more while taking in the view. The more I interacted with Lauren, the greater I began recognizing we are like chalk and cheese. She grew up in a rural area around horses, without much exposure to the flashing lights of a big city. She engaged in what I assumed was self-deprecating humor at the end of the phrase telling us about herself, where she said, "You sound like such a worldly person Neha, I'm basically white trash." I didn't quite know how to respond to that.

Luckily I didn't need to say anything as we pulled into Via San Francesco a Ripa, the street that housed our new home. The area had so much character- there was a cornetto and gelato shop right by our apartment, with a bar next to it. A grocery store and hookah bar that would later become our favorite hangout was down the street and the neighborhood was dotted with cafe's, vendors, pizzerias, casual Italian restaurants called osterias and trattorias. We heard two lovers squabble in Italian as vespas whizzed past and saw that two steps away from us the street opened out into Piazza Santa Maria, which habited a magnificent fountain and church. Everywhere we looked there was something going on, and it only got better in the evenings when a young crowd flocked to the bar after work and the street-side accordion players and performers added to the color.

Our apartment was in a little building, on the second floor. When I walked into our home, I couldn't believe how large it was! It was a nice space with an open kitchen, a small dining table and a couch tossed to the side making it a living room cum kitchen. There was a washing machine in the bathroom. The best part though, was that each one of us had our own room with a beautiful balcony overlooking the street below us. We could see the bar, the piazza, the lovers. "I feel like Juliet, and this is my Rome-Rome-Romeo," Ada exclaimed as she stepped out into her balcony with open arms. I had to agree with her as I too fell instantly in love with my surroundings. We were the only set of students in the program where each person got their own room within the apartment. We were literally in the middle of all the action in Trastevere, a few minutes away from the Tiber, the third longest river in Italy that runs through the middle of Rome. Small little things we discovered along the way also made us feel like we were the most privileged three in our study abroad program. Prior to leaving, we were all warned that using dryers after washing clothes was not a common practice in Italy. We were mentally prepared to dry all our laundry by hanging out our clothes on a clothesline tied up to the window. Three days into the program, little Miss Ada toys around with the washer and says, "Hey guys, this machine looks a little too sophisticated. There are so many settings, what do I use to wash my clothes without shrinking them or messing up?" She used Google Translate and figured out that one of the options on our washer, 'asciugatura' actually meant "to dry" in Italian. "Oh my God," she said, "Ohmygodohmygodohmygod I think we have a dryer!" she exclaimed. "Lauren, Neha come here and check this out. If I turn the knob this way, I think the dryer starts!" Indeed we were the only three in the program who had the rare luxury of a built-in dryer. It is amazing - when you are out of your comfort zone, you value all the little things you tend to take for granted in your home surroundings.

A parallel from the Semester at Sea program comes to mind. During our first day in South Africa, my friends complained that the Oreos they purchased in Cape Town didn't taste half as good as American Oreos, and that the brand needed to be more globally consistent. Four days of exposure to poverty and an overnight visit to a traditional African township made them realize that the world has bigger problems than catering to cookie-snobs. In any case, people tend to be actively aware of the adjustments that they are making when away from their home surroundings.

I spent the next two weeks inhaling Rome and familiarizing myself with my new home and the people around me. I walked the streets lining the Tiber river, made cappuccino pit -stops in little bakeries, bathed myself in the chocolate and hazelnut gelatos (all in moderation of course!), made it to the major historic sites and got all the touristy things out of the way before I really started to experience Rome as a resident. In due time I also picked out my friends from the group. Matt, Ada and I got along naturally, and I was quite fond of Johnny too. John McDonough was a wonderfully raised kid whose parents live in the city of Chicago. He was fun-loving and adventurous enough such that we planned our weekend trips to Milan and Amsterdam together with Matt. The four of us became a group the first week, and Lauren would hang out with us too. Most of the time this was only because she lived with us and happened to be there, and couldn't quite bring herself to interact frequently with the twenty other kids in our program. She was quiet most of the time, the listener of the group while Ada and I were the talkers. It worked well in making us a cohesive unit. Funnily enough, the very differences between Lauren and me are what made me begin to care about her. While opening up to us about her personal life, Lauren confessed that she had been in a steady relationship, but her boyfriend who was also studying abroad in Paris wanted to take a break while they were abroad and maybe get back together once they returned to the States. Ada and I were shocked when she told us. "Well isn't that convenient?" asked Ada, "He can try being with other girls, guilt-free while he's away from you and then have you right back when he wants it. Sounds like this guy likes to have his cake and eat it too."

"Yes Lauren," I added, "it doesn't sound like he really cares about you. You said that you wanted to be with him; three months isn't a long time, and you are only a couple of hours away from each other. It shouldn't be that hard to stay committed and visit each other while abroad. In all honesty, I wouldn't take that. I'd give him an all or nothing ultimatum, otherwise how will he ever respect you or take your relationship seriously in the long run? He'll always assume its fine to pull an on or off switch on you, which isn't okay."

She agreed with what we had to say, but couldn't help herself. She was clearly in love with this guy and told him that it was alright for them to not be in a relationship while abroad, but that they would still be friends and visit each other and then get back together once they returned to college. She even had her trip to Paris lined up in a few weeks to visit him 'as friends'. Right.

Even though it was none of my business, it made me so upset to think that my roommate was being taken for granted. I had become protective of Lauren and was determined to ensure that she didn't waste her time brooding over this boyfriend while in Rome. She didn't need to care for him as much as she did, and quite frankly, I didn't need to be around someone who was moping while I intended to have the time of my life during this once in a lifetime opportunity.

I wanted to interact with locals, explore the city and have fun while I studied this majestic civilization. With that frame of mind, Ada and I met a friendly bunch of Italian students in the piazza during our first weekend. Upon learning that we were new to Rome, they offered to show our group around and explore together. We took them up on their offer, and the next night they took us all to Vista, a prominent rooftop nightclub. It was up on a little hill right by the Colosseum, with a gorgeous view of the city. So it turns out that there was indeed a colorful nightlife to be found amidst the ruins...We dragged Lauren out with us saying that we were here just for ten weeks, which meant that we should look beautiful, feel like twenty-one year olds and go every night if possible. She said that she hadn't really had much exposure to clubbing before, but was curious to experience it. The three of us got ready together, borrowed each other's make up and accessories and dressed like we deserved to live in Italy. We teetered down the narrow, cobblestoned path in our high heels feeling an unfamiliar pain in our ankles but it was worth it. We ended up having a blast - dancing, meeting people and getting Lauren a few drinks. It began raining but that just made our night all the better. People didn't let the rain stop them and continued dancing out on the open roof as the DJ spun popular house music tracks. We got drenched, laughed in amazement as the party raved on and we bobbed our wet hair from side to side and sang to the music without a care in the world. While we were dancing I also happened to click a few pictures of our group with the Italian boys.

The next day, I woke up and trudged out of my room with a mildly sore throat. When I came out, Lauren had cups of coffee ready for the both of us. She had experimented with the Mokapot, the traditional Italian stovetop coffee maker in our apartment and prepared strong espressos to go with breakfast. We sat down and she told me about how much fun she had clubbing. "Lets do this more often," she said. Little did she know that I had already planned our next night out. I bonded with Lauren as she gushed, and I decided that I was henceforth going to make her a part of all my social plans. I had begun to accept her and really like her. It was refreshing to hear someone gush about activities that were routine to my friends and I back at home.

We live in the digital age, and social media has become the new way to interact with friends, make new ones and cement friendships. I logged onto my Facebook, instantly uploaded our pictures from the previous night and put in a few sweet captions to accompany pictures of Lauren and myself to express my newfound affection for her. The (not so) great thing about social media is that your family, friends and your friends' friends can all see exactly what you're up to. I tagged Lauren in all my photos, and made sure that pictures of her with the boys showed up on her wall. Somewhere inside me I hoped that her now-we-are-on-now-we-are-off-boyfriend would spot these pictures and notice that while he chose to temporarily drop her, she was out having a great time the very first weekend.

As time progressed, Lauren began coming out of her shell. It was delightful to see her transform as she borrowed my purses and accessories, altered her dressing sense saying she couldn't really go out looking like a retired school teacher. She was letting us, and the highly fashionable, impeccably attired people in Italy influence her sense of dressing positively and although she only made minor changes, she appeared like a completely different person to me. She began to come across as distinctive and fun-loving and I began noticing traits in her that I really admired.

Despite having grown up in a rural area, she was the most street smart out of our group of five. She navigated her way around the complex, confusing city and helped us find our way out whenever we felt lost. I realized I did have a few things in common with her- we both liked to run, and bonded over going for long runs along the Tiber the rest of that quarter. On one afternoon, we decided to give ourselves an uphill, interval workout by training through some of the hills in Rome. We got lost on our way to the Villa Borghese, and ended up witnessing a traditional wedding at a villa atop the hill. It was a beautiful ceremony, taking place against the most breathtaking backdrop: with the ancient city below them, these two people vowed to spend the rest of their lives loving one another. It was highly romantic and beauty in its simplest form. I began to dream of my own wedding being an intimate, cozy affair in beautiful Italy as opposed to the cheerful, big, loud, week long Indian-style colorful celebration I will most likely have. Lauren and I paused, caught our breath, witnessed the moment and exchanged smiles. We needed no words to share that memorable moment. Our friendship began cementing as we enjoyed unique incidents like these in a foreign land together.

For one of our classes we had to make an on-site presentation, and Lauren and I chose to pair up and present Rafael's frescos and the Sistine Chapel when our class visited the Vatican. It was the most inspiring learning environment to say the least, to be surrounded by Rafael's masterpieces as we discussed them. Our group reveled in the love of learning together, absorbing culture with all our senses. Our wonderful professors Cam Hawkins and Christina Von Nolcken took our group on several educational trips to Pompei, Naples and Florence. Roman history came alive as we learnt about the gladiators at the Colosseum, and had classes at the Forum and the Pantheon. We developed an appreciation of the place religion held in people's lives by visiting a series of breathtaking chapels, basilicas and cathedrals. Observing the workmanship in art, architecture or artifacts, be it the usage of gold or the intricate manner in which the Virgin Mary has been depicted through stained glass art gave our learning a perspective that simply cannot be created in a classroom. Apart from our coursework, we would take personal weekend trips as well. I loved observing (and engaging in) celebrations such as the Perugia Eurochocolate Festival or Sagra Dell'uva, the Wine and Grape Festival in Marino. Marino is a small town in the Lazio region of Italy that is renowned for its wine production. Every year there is a festival where the entire town gets converted into a ridiculously lively street carnival. Bottles of wine are sold for 4 Euros per liter and food and balloon vendors take over the town as locals and tourists indulge. There is a marching band, a parade, music everywhere, dancing and the main attraction is a large fountain that spills out wine for the day. Ada, Lauren, Matt and I took off on a train to Marino at the Termini station in Rome, and ended the day collectively cringing yet laughing at the drunk people vomit off a cliff in the not-so-quaint-anymore town or on the train tracks as we waited for our ride back to Rome.

I took pleasure in discovering more about Lauren and realized the folly of judging a book by its cover. As I scratched beneath the surface, I learnt that she was the most kind, generous person I'd met in my life. Each and every night she would go grocery shopping and cook our friend's group-of-five a fancy dinner of delicious risottos, pastas and deserts. After dinner, we would have to force her to sit down and let us wash the dishes as she claimed she loved both cooking and cleaning up after. She entertained us with her precious one-liners and incredible sense of humor. She went from being the awkward outsider in our friends' circle to cementing us as a family; I began to love her like a best friend or family member.

While we were in the process of deepening our bonds, Ada played to her strengths by being the extroverted, socially active friend. One weekend she visited her friend in Florence who told us to get in touch with Alfredo, a local club promoter who invited us out to clubs, parties and took wonderful care of us. She found and booked us apartments to live in while traveling over the weekends, and was always supportive of my adventurous ideas to go out for late night walks or to attempt to do our Italian homework at a local hangout on a Tuesday night. She came with me to the delectable bakeries and we would relish hazelnut biscotti and decadent hot chocolates. Between Ada and Lauren, I had everything I could ever want. A small part of me still believes that God sent them into my life as my guardian angels: although I was in totally unfamiliar territory with totally unfamiliar people, their friendship, love and care cushioned me and gave me a strong sense of security. I still consider those ten weeks in Rome to be the most perfect ten weeks of my life.

To this day, they are my best friends. When I was transitioning between apartments back in Chicago and needed a place to stay for a few weeks, Ada let me into hers instead of allowing me to sublet an apartment. She generously offered that I sleep on her bed and use her bathroom and living space for as long as I wanted. She said that my home was hers, and joked that I occupied less room than her boyfriend. Lauren too continued to cook me the most delicious meals back in Chicago. She remembered my favorite vegetable- butternut squash- and frequently called me over whenever she made that particular risotto. She used chocolate and peanut butter, my two favorite foods and experimented baking delicious pies for me. On my birthday, she presented me with a large, most luscious chocolate cake, which made me feel like Bruce Bogtrotter, a chubby little child from my favorite childhood book Matilda. Matt too engaged my love of sweets and brought me macaroons. Apart from feeding me, my strangers-turned-good friends always give me valuable life advice regarding career prospects, genuinely caring for me with all their heart.

Ada and Lauren were two different personalities- I clicked instantly with one, and took a while to become friends with the other. If there's one thing I learnt from my friendship with Lauren, it is that true gems can emerge once polishing past the surface. At that time, it was important for me to step outside my bubble of judgement and learn how to give people a fair chance with an open mind. You never know who can surprise you, and even today I continue to be surprised by the people I encounter on my travels.

College is the ideal time to learn to get out of one's social comfort zone. It is a platform to date all types of people and make friends from diverse walks of life, as campuses in the United States generally tend to possess a vibrant mix of people. My other two friends in the Rome group, Matt and Johnny were both all-American boys, while I generally tended to befriend international girls. However, the way in which our friendship developed was unique. I could share things with them that I did not with my female friends. On our weekend trip to Milan together, I had enlightening discussions about life and politics and learnt how to appreciate a different sense of humor. Back in Chicago, I met their wonderful families, observed contrasts in the ways in which we were raised and bridged many cultural gaps through our mutual love of food and travel. It made me truly experience pluralism and realize that relationships are enriched with diversity, if one is open and can appreciate the inherent good in others. As one of my friends on the Semester at Sea program shared in a speech, "From the outside, it is too easy to make judgements about those who are different....to hold stereotypes. Us and them. But when we sit down together, the differences in our values, in our beliefs, in our assumptions that looked so divisive from the outside begin to be seen more as interesting variations because we discover that there is so much more that we share."

My advice to every about-to-be freshman or college student: please use the opportunities at hand to open yourself up and burst your comfort zone bubble. Interact with people who aren't like you, date someone you don't typically think is your type. The amount you will learn both about the world and yourself, and grow as a result is tremendous. If possible, travel through a study abroad program and meet international students to gain maximum cultural depth. Learning about a culture by experiencing a way of life with a local can be the most authentic experience. My roommate during my senior year, Itir, who is from Turkey oftentimes cooked me the most delicious foods- Dolma, spiced rice wrapped in leaves, and frequently shared sweet pistachio Turkish Delights that her parents sent her. I got to interact with her Turkish friends, and understand more about their culture and political approach during the Diren Gezi protests last year. Itir's best friend, Ekin, who also happened to be Ada's boyfriend is a Turk who told me the funniest stories about his country, and elements of his culture that he loved. My Brazilian friends Catarina, Nicole and Joana always organized the Carnaval festival celebration on our campus in Chicago, which had lots of samba dancing and delicious food. On a day-to-day basis we often got together as I watched them prepare Brigadeiro from scratch. Food and gastronomical exploration aside, I often held conversations about religious and social life, festivals and functions and compared life in Bahrain to life in Mumbai with my dear friends Faisal and Abdulla. These opportunities to learn through interaction, without having to read a book or magazine or watch the news are special. Believe me when I say it is worth reaping the benefits of diversity: I not only ate delicious foods from around the world, but also now have homes to stay in a handful of countries with the friends I made for life. Most valuable of all, however, is the broadening of my vistas and fundamental change in my personality that came about from bouncing out of my comfort zone.

CHAPTER 7
Meeting Yourself

"Travel far enough, you meet yourself."
- David Mitchell, Cloud Atlas

Who am I? What do I stand for? What is my purpose? What do I do next? College particularly, is that critical phase when one metamorphoses from a teenager into a young adult and tends to reflect upon such questions in an endeavor to define oneself. The exposure in college through Rome and studying abroad led to my next step – a step that changed my life! I discovered that this earth is a spellbinding place and being young is a great time to be shocked, surprised, overwhelmed, inspired and taught about the ways of the world. It was this sentiment that inspired me to apply for the Semester At Sea (SAS) program.

I learnt about SAS through the National Society of High School Scholars (NSHSS), an academic honour society that I have been a member of since high school. The NSHSS does some admirable work in connecting its student members to resources and opportunities to help them build on academic success. As a result, they partner with various organizations, the Semester at Sea program being one of them. One fine day I received an informational email from the NSHSS informing members of the upcoming voyage and learning opportunities. I sent in an application, and was thrilled to get accepted.

Soon after graduating, I spent a semester learning at sea and sailing across the globe with over five hundred other students. We sailed through Russia, Germany, Belgium, France, Ireland, Portugal, Spain, Morocco, Ghana, South Africa and around the rim of the Atlantic to Argentina, Brazil, Cuba and the Bahamas. Time in ports included engaging in cultural and humanitarian activities helping us understand structural and social changes taking place in the world. The experience offered students an ideal combination of classroom learning provided by professors on board the MV Explorer and experiential learning through activities at port. As Marcel Proust says, *"The real voyage of discovery consists not in seeking new landscapes, but in having new eyes."*

Often, tourism exposes people to experiences that shake one up and give one a new perspective on life. We happily engaged in various enriching activities at port. I had the unique opportunity to voice my views on Child Trafficking at a Human Rights Commission event, when we made a trip to the Palais Des Nations, the United Nations headquarters in Geneva. Additionally, we were also exposed to some soul-stirring experiences. Let me narrate the saddest one I have known.

Our ship docked at Ghana, and we students were taken to visit the Elmina and Cape Coast castles. President Obama and his family visited the Cape Coast Castle in July 2009. These castles had been built by the British, Dutch and Portuguese, who governed colonies in Africa, to serve as warehouses to store commodities and spices for trade. They then slowly began to trade Africans as slaves. We saw the dungeons at the basement of the castles in which the slaves were held – two hundred slaves in a room chained to each other so they couldn't move. There was one tiny window for ventilation for two hundred odd people who lived, slept and attended the calls of nature in the same room. They were fed twice a day, and all they could eat was what they could fit in their palms. That's it. It was hot, smelly and disgusting. We were told about how they were lashed and punished, and how governors handpicked women slaves who were then raped by them. If the women resisted and refused to be raped, they were beaten and thrown into a closed, dark, unventilated cell where they were left to suffocate to death. I saw nail scratch marks on the walls made by people struggling for breath, on the brink of suffocation. The slaves that survived the dungeon were made to walk, in shackles, through the "Door of No Return" which was a door that led out open onto the beach where ships would dock and transport them off to faraway lands to work as slaves in plantations. That was the last time they would ever set foot on African soil. A captain of one of these boats was recorded as saying, "The slaves felt as free as a man feels in his coffin." Seeing the dungeons and understanding the history of the slave trade was very traumatic. I never felt so ashamed to be a human being as I did that day: I was shocked at the things that we as a race are capable of. President Barack Obama summed up the emotions one feels when one visits the slave dungeons quite aptly when he said that a slave site reminded him of Nazi concentration camps. It was a reminder of humanity's potential for "great evil" but also gives a reason for hope, given the progress African-Americans have made since leaving the castle as slaves.

That day was solemn, and even the beautiful Cape Coastline drive back to our ship in Tema didn't manage to cheer me up. One thing that did resonate with me, however, is the peaceful attitude that the Ghanians have towards their history. They've come to terms with what happened and as we left the dungeons there was a sign that our tour guide read aloud, "The color of one's skin doesn't matter, all that matters is that this incident in history never happens again." Locals claim that President Obama was touched when his daughters walked through the Door of No Return and then walked back in, their gesture symbolic of the progress and evolution of humankind. Much as it shocked me, I am glad to have had this experience, particularly because my glasses tended to have that over-critical lens when examining minor issues. This incident drove home the realization that there are bigger problems that people have historically faced, dealt with and overcome.

Going back to an old home after spending time away will almost certainly make you feel like the place has changed. In most cases, the place won't have changed so much as your lens and way of viewing it. There is a story about a fish in a fishbowl. There is a way in which a fish swimming around in a fishbowl knows nothing at all about water because water is so much a part of the fish's life. It is surrounded by water. It is embedded in water. In that sense, the fish does not really know water. If you want the fish to really understand water, you have to take the fish out of the fishbowl and say, "Look, that's water." Now, if you put the fish back in, the water never looks the same again. New experiences add perspective, and change the ways in which one views and interacts with people. To emphasize this, let me quote Andrew Gray, a friend from Semester At Sea, with a reflection of the impact that our voyage had on him. Andrew dis-embedded himself from his life in Oklahoma and seamlessly interacted with people outside of his home bubble.

"How do I put the last four months into words? I saw the ocean for the first time; then lived on it for four months. I left the country for the first time and went to 16 other countries each one more amazing than the last. I met incredible people, including a Nobel Laureate, the minister to Nelson Mandela on Robben Island, The Vice-President of Hamburg, Germany's Parliament, two NASA astronauts, not to mention countless amazing young people that are ready to take on their new dreams, opportunities and to use their talents to change this world we live in. I went and saw the work that Pencils Of Promise (a prominent global non-governmental organization) does every single day in communities around the world and got to experience a day at the United Nations in Geneva, Switzerland. But much more than all of this, what I am humbled, honored, blessed, and overly excited about remembering and reflecting on is not the countries, the events, the newspapers, the cuban cigars, or anything like this. What inspired and motivated me and what I learned the most from are the friendships and relationships I made with people from all around the world, of different ages, cultures, races, genders, beliefs and causes, and how I can keep in contact with these people and have them help to continually change my life. I will miss everyone that I had the opportunity to glean knowledge, wisdom, inspiration, and just a general excitement to change the world from and I know that this day is not a day to say goodbye and it isn't even the end of our journeys.

This is the beginning of a whole new chapter in our lives. A chapter when we take what we learned, who we learned from and we make something of it. Sure, some of us may hope to build schools around the world for the rest of our lives. Some of us may want to be doctors, lawyers, social workers, CEOs of Fortune 500 companies; some of us may want a job with Semester at Sea, some of us may want to be artists, Hollywood directors or actors, some of us may even want to travel the world taking opportunities at small time jobs just to have the ability to continue traveling; some of us may even hope to be plumbers. But I know that if each one of us does something that we love, if each one of us places our time and our passions into something that we care about deeply, then it will never be the end for us. Those were the moments that I realized I needed to be a part of something bigger than myself, and who knows, maybe those will be the moments when we look back and say - those were the moments that for the first time in our lives, we found ourselves."

Being abroad inspired Andrew to discover his passion and follow his interests and he now works with Pencils of Promise empowering young people through education around the globe. They are currently working towards building a school. Being away provided him with the opportunity to evaluate his life from a fresh lens.

Another instance that reaffirmed my faith in the potential of humankind was our trip to Cuba. Here is my Facebook post after embarking from the port:

> "I'm not one to typically post long, political statuses, but this is a cool story. A few days ago I was fortunate enough to experience history. My ship very skeptically added Cuba as a port of call, despite facing much trouble from the US State Department. As most Americans are not allowed to visit Cuba unless on an education trip like ours, it was significant that our cruise docked in the waters of Havana and let hundreds of Americans venture off into a nation out of their political comfort zone.
>
> Cuba and the USA have very strained relations both historically and through the embargo in present day. The socio-political relations of both nations filter through to a micro level: US credit cards don't work in Cuba, there is no American cell phone service and we all had to pull out our leftover Euros as dollars aren't the commonly exchanged currency form. You don't see American tourists in Cuba- they're not allowed by their government.
>
> We arrived not knowing what to expect, but stepped off the ship to find individual gift bags for all 600 of us from the Cubans. Diplomats and Ambassadors often like to come on board in countries and talk to students since we're on a unique international mission, and the first thing that the Cuban officials told us is that Cubans know how to distinguish between Americans and their government. They have a great respect for the American people and said that after a long gap of seeing no American students, they were ready to welcome them into their country.
>
> There was a mandatory special program arranged for all students at the University of Havana, which had an unbelievable amount of media attention. Cuban and American students gathered in their historic old square listening to their Dean and our Deans and other dignitaries addressing

thousands saying that despite what happened in the past, what is important is that we're all here today, together, united, forming positive relations with one another and connecting on a human level. They waved their wands and magically spread love in the air. That afternoon had presentations by American History and law professors from UH to educate all the students about the history and why the two governments have sour relations. The takeaway we received was that there are two sides to every story and although this is important to understanding moving forward we must release negativity and judgements to take steps towards peace and fostering healthy economic relations in future.

As we made our way back to the ship, my American friend smiled and said, "I never thought I'd come to Cuba, and drink mojitos and Cuba libres with actual Cubans in my life... I can't believe I'm here." We didn't just go to their university and express peace but took our newfound friendships out of that square. Through the two days that we were there, groups of Cuban students bent themselves backwards taking us to their local amphitheater, a baseball game, hot spots such as cigar factories and prominent museums and on our last night they organized a party for all the students at one of Havana's popular nightclubs. They made sure that every student on that ship knew that Cubans were a warm, welcoming, nonjudgmental group of people that didn't care what anybody's government told its people- they just wanted to have a good time. As we pulled away from the harbour, hundreds of students waited in the terminal next to both American and Cuban flags, waving and shouting while we stood outdoors and waved back, not wanting to leave as many didn't know if they would ever be allowed to re-visit Cuba in their lifetime.

I'm not American so I probably didn't experience the same range of emotional intensity I saw in some of my American friends that day. It was, however, heartwarming to watch this incredible expression of warmth and togetherness from both ends and be part of the movement taken towards bridging country relations at a micro level. Despite being in some very dark places and seeing the best and worst of our world in the last four months- be it concentration camps in Germany, consequences of the apartheid in Cape Town or slave dungeons in Ghana, which gave me nightmares for a week after I departed, it is incidents like these that make me believe in humanity and think that my generation is amazing. We have so much potential."

Classrooms will provide academic knowledge, extracurricular activities will add skills. However venturing and wandering into unfamiliar territory is what will lead to the maximum personal growth as an individual…it gives us the chance to discover ourselves. The catch with this is that the initiative and desire to seek such experiences has to come purely from within. Classes will incentivize performance with grades, and a leadership position in an activity may serve as the dangling carrot to inspire performance. Breaking away from your bubble is something you need to do yourself without knowledge of the potential pay offs. I'm hoping that some of my experiences will serve as a springboard to inspire students to venture out of your social and geographic comfort zones while in college. It hasn't even been a year out of college and I don't remember half the classes I took or the grades I received for them. But what I will always remember is how Chicago grew to become home, how I spent ten amazing weeks in Rome and four very enriching months living on a ship after graduation. Those are the stories that make up the treasure chest I hold so close to my heart and will someday narrate to my grandchildren.

CHAPTER 8

Habits for Creating an Active and Rewarding Social Life

"You can't cross the sea merely by standing and staring at the water."
- Rabindranath Tagore

One of my favorite quotes, this line of Tagore-wisdom can be applied to multiple dimensions of life. The payoffs of pro-activeness extend past academic and professional settings to even the smallest of social scenarios. I learnt this lesson early on.

It was my first year in college and I was still residing in the dorms. One fine morning my roommate Julianne says to me, "Neha, guess what? I just heard that Bill Gates is coming to UChicago in two weeks!"

"What!?" I exclaimed, "THE Bill Gates? As in, one of the richest people on earth is coming to our school? Why?"

"I'm not sure...I think he's coming to give a talk. Probably about Microsoft, his foundation or both. I've heard that there is going to be quite a spectacle at Rockefeller Chapel."

Grand, historic and overwhelmingly magnificent, Rockefeller Chapel is the ceremonial and spiritual center at the University of Chicago. It serves witness to most major events and addresses during Orientation and Convocation as it is an excellent location to accommodate hundreds of people. It resembles a medieval cathedral and its tall arches reverberate with the powerful sounds of the organ and choir during services. I was excited to hear that Mr. Gates, yet another renowned personality, was going to be speaking in the chapel soon.

We found out through official sources that Mr. Gates would be addressing students on how the brightest minds can address some of the biggest global problems. Us bright minds were eagerly awaiting Mr. Gates' arrival and we began counting down the days to his visit. When the day finally arrived, I distractedly got through my work and as evening dawned, walked over to 59th street and South University Avenue where Rockefeller Chapel is located. There was already a long-winding line of people waiting to enter, that stretched across five blocks as hundreds of students wanted to glean from Mr. Gates' wisdom. I sighed deeply as I got in line. The queue continued to grow behind me as more students showed up, extending all the way through campus buildings. Forty minutes later, I finally managed to set foot in the chapel. My eyes rapidly scanned the room to find a good spot but all seats in the student area were already occupied. People were crowding around the corners guarding a minuscule amount of territory in an attempt to make room to stand. The chapel continued to fill up as students kept pouring in.

    People settled down as the clock kept ticking and soon it would be time for Mr. Gates to arrive. The manner in which the crowd thronged was akin to the density of population one witnesses at a rock concert! I thought to myself that I would be lucky if I even found a little space to stand a visible distance away from the stage. I noticed a little bit of room by one of the pillars closer to the front and made my way towards it. When I inched closer, I realized why the spot had been empty. There was a huge pillar that obstructed the view of the stage! I walked forward in an attempt to salvage whatever I could see when all of a sudden my eyes caught an empty seat far off in the second row, behind the Deans and dignitaries. It didn't look like it was taken, as there was no bag or coat placed over it. The first ten or so rows were blocked off as reserved seating, so students were only allowed to occupy the seats after the reserved area. "What a waste of an incredible seat," I thought to myself as I stood in the corner. I noticed the lady who was guarding the blocked section. She looked a little friendly. I found myself wondering why not take a chance and ask her if it would be possible for me to slip into that lonely chair up front. I was feeling a little nervous, but I mustered up the courage and walked up to her. At the most, I would have to face a rejection, which would leave me in no worse position than I currently was in but if she agreed I had a lot to gain with practically nothing to lose!

    "Excuse me," I said, "if that chair over there is empty, would it be possible for me to sneak in and occupy it?"

    "I'm sorry," she said, "those seats aren't for students."

    My face fell a little. "Okay," I piped in, "But if it is still empty in a few minutes and you change your mind I'll be standing right here. And believe me, you'd make my day by changing your mind. So please, please consider it. Besides, it is going to look so bad to have an empty seat in the second row! Think about it..."

    I cocked my head and threw my sweetest, most charming smile at her. Looking at me, her face softened and she smiled back. She seemed to have some reservations but whispered, "Give it a few minutes and if no one shows up I'll let you around the corner. But you have to be quiet about it!" (And quiet I was about it, that is, until I decided to write this book)

I nervously stepped back a little and went into the corner. I kept glancing around in anticipation. A few minutes later, much to my good fortune the seat was still unoccupied. I looked around and up at the woman, and as soon as she caught my eye I smiled again. After about five minutes of stares from me demonstrating my longing to get through, she finally tilted her head indicating that I could come around.

I bolted forward as she swiftly released the ropes blocking the section. I walked up front and took the seat literally seconds before Mr. Gates was introduced. I couldn't believe how close to the podium I was sitting: me, a little freshman nobody, sitting amidst dignitaries only a few meters away from one of the richest, most successful leaders of the world. Robert Zimmer, the President of the University of Chicago introduced Bill Gates who began his enlightening talk. It was an amazing experience watching him speak up close, addressing important issues such as poverty, education and global health and taking in the wisdom he offered to our student body. I listened with a keen ear because having grown up and lived in a developing nation, these are issues that have been of concern to me. Wanting to make a difference in whatever little way I can, my broader goal in life is to make a meaningful impact and help those in need. It doesn't matter whether I manage to make a small or significant difference, whether I serve in the east or the west, but I would certainly like to improve the quality of human life for those people who are victims of poverty. Listening to a world leader share concrete ideas about ways in which I can actualize my goal, was fruitful. As I was seated so close to the stage and the topic of the address was close to my heart, I oftentimes felt like Mr. Gates was addressing me directly. Consequently, a few minutes after the talk I had the opportunity to start an interesting conversation with the woman seated next to me, who was an employee at the Bill and Melinda Gates Foundation. I chatted with her in detail about philanthropic endeavors of the foundation and was impressed by the breadth of issues they covered. Seeing as I had numerous questions about how youth could contribute, she discussed the possibility of summer internships and left me her business card as she had to leave and escort Mr. Gates out of the chapel. I couldn't believe how exceptionally well this experience had turned out. As I walked away from the chapel, I vowed to nurture an outgoing, proactive trait within me. Although this is a very small example, it taught me one of the most important lessons of my college life: *If you see something that you want, go for it. What may seem out of your reach may very well be within it.*

    I'm certain that many students spotted that empty seat in Rockefeller Chapel, but were probably too scared, nervous or simply felt they didn't belong and dismissed the idea of asking to sit there. Ultimately, however the student who cared enough to ask and persisted managed to attain it. *Being able to make the things you want happen isn't easy. But without taking the initiative or even trying, a difficult task, by default, becomes impossible.* In the words of Chinese philosopher Lao Tzu, "A journey of a thousand miles begins with a single step".

    Pro-activeness serves a college student well in most facets of life. Being an energetic, outgoing persona will help you make tons of friends, find out about events and carve a niche for yourself on campus. Professionally, an important connection could assist in the job or internship process and can sometimes change the course of life, irrespective of field. One of my friends that worked with me as a Career Peer Adviser secured a finance internship in New York through an alumna that was in her sorority. The funny thing is that she wasn't even interested in banking, but talking to this woman at a social get-together and learning more about the industry opened her eyes. Consequently, she managed to put her foot in the job door quite easily thanks to her connection. Making the most of your experience is going to require all the energy you have but the payoffs are worth it. Students are young creatures bubbling with energy, and with good reason. College can be draining both mentally during midterms or finals season, and physically on weekends when late nights out have turned into early mornings as students stumble back to their residences still awake but dreaming of their beds. Time is truly a rare commodity, and the only way to fit multiple pursuits in and accomplish considerably is to be on the move. Having too much free time could be indicative of a waste of one's potential. Besides, paradoxical as it may seem, I find that people who are dynamic in several areas of their life manage to achieve more in an individual pursuit as compared to a relatively inactive person. There is something about the mindset of staying functional and achieving goals: it is best to utilize one's energy and be on the move.

I was discussing the merits of pro-activeness with a group of friends, when one of them asked, "What if I am too introverted to ask for the things that I want or take initiative in conversation?" It can be difficult for some people to be social, and this is perfectly understandable. For natural extroverts like myself, talking comes more easily as we like directing our energy outwards. It isn't necessary to have a large social circle and constantly talk to people, but I believe that it is important to know and find out what is going on in one's community. The internet can facilitate this, but simply opening your mouth and connecting with people verbally can provide value and insight that is often difficult to find through other means. It is perfectly reasonable to have a fear of rejection, or a fear of looking silly if one is declined, but in most normal situations it pays to ask yourself the question: *What do I have to lose if I'm told 'no', and what do I stand to gain if I'm told 'yes'? Are the payoffs going to exceed what I have to potentially lose?* Sometimes simply reminding oneself of this can be incentive enough to approach someone in seeking a pursuit. Additionally, utilizing email, social media or the multiple text and chat platforms our generation has at its disposal today is an excellent way to approach and connect, if one does not want to initiate a conversation in person or needs time to think through responses.

For what it's worth, I've been fortunate in that most people I've encountered in the world are nice, and like to help others especially if it doesn't cost them more than a bit of time or effort. It leads me to believe that people are inherently good and it is great to be able to tap into that goodness. A lot of times people miss out on getting the things that they want because they didn't take the trouble to ask.

Ask. I attained many things that I wanted simply by asking. During my third year, I was dining at iNG, a famous molecular gastronomy restaurant run by renowned chef Homaro Cantu in Chicago. Molecular gastronomy explores the social, technical and artistic components of food creation using scientific innovations to create modernist cuisine. Surreal and thought provoking dishes are brought to the table embodying a taste changing experience. Dishes visually appear as one thing but taste like something completely different. iNG for example, prides itself on the 'miracle berry'. This little marvel is a naturally grown substance that possesses the capability to transform one's tastebuds to perceive an increased sweetness in foods. I went to iNG with two of my best friends, Catarina and Amanda and our minds were blown upon consuming the berry and a wedge of lime after. What should have been sour and unappealing tasted like a freshly plucked orange from Andalusian Spain! I asked for about three wedges of lime to chew on because I couldn't believe the potential of this berry. We then tasted course after course of decadent deserts after our tastebuds had been influenced by the truly miraculous 'miracle berry'. We enjoyed the unique, innovative creations that were presented in the most artistic ways with specially created beverage pairings. In fact, I grew to become so passionate about molecular gastronomy that I would frequent similar establishments when I felt like I could afford a bit of splurging. There was a huge presence of this modern cuisine in Chicago and it began to fascinate me. When I returned to iNG a few months later I spoke with Trevor, the manager, after my meal. I expressed my enthusiasm to learn more about this form of cuisine and casually mentioned that I would love to intern with them for a few months. He asked me to stay in touch, and I followed up. A few months later, I was an employee at iNG.

I spent three months engaging a passion and learning about the restaurant and service industry. I assisted with a variety of tasks in kitchen management and learnt the nuanced graces of fine dining. This experience opened my eyes to the detail one needs to take in order to attain perfection while demanding that I acquire a totally new skill-set. The kind of challenges the University of Chicago had conditioned me to, were typically demanding papers that required hours and all-nighters in the library, not running around a restaurant learning to creatively fold napkins, assist chefs, or prepare a bar before a busy evening of service. I learnt what it means to have a great organizational culture and it redefined my understanding of customer service. I'm so grateful for this fantastic experience that also taught me people-skills. I wouldn't have been able to gain this opportunity if I hadn't taken a risk and asked if I could work at iNG.

Connect. You are as powerful as your network. The ability to both form and tap connections at the apt time can transform one's social stature, in addition to being an indispensable tool while finding jobs. The merits of forming new connections particularly helped me while studying abroad. In Rome, Ada and I would often strike up a conversation with locals and inquire about the best restaurants, nightclubs and city spots to explore. We were two ordinary students on a study abroad program and just by conversing with a friend who was concurrently studying abroad in Florence, Ada managed to navigate her way into high-society Italian nightlife. Ada's friend connected her with a promoter in Rome, and this was the turning point as far as social life in Rome was concerned.

Before we made acquaintances, we had tried gaining admission into an exclusive nightclub called White on our first weekend out. We unfortunately weren't granted entry as there was a big crowd waiting outside this elite establishment. Oh, the heartbreak of facing rejection, however minor... When Ada called Alfredo, the Roman promoter her friend had introduced her to he invited us to the club that he was promoting for the evening. Surprise, Surprise; turns out it was White! Upon arriving we were pulled up by a bouncer to cut the line following which we were escorted straight to the VIP section. Alfredo had also arranged an elaborate bottle service for our friends' circle, which we weren't expecting as newbies in a foreign nation. Although I personally do not consume alcohol and am happy enough to simply enjoy the aspect of being young and out dancing, Ada, Johnny, Lauren and Matt were absolutely thrilled. Needless to say, our lives in Rome were never the same.

We went from being strangers in a city, to dancing among its most elite. Alfredo was hospitable and invited our entire friend group to other parties he hosted, such as a huge Halloween celebration at Atlantico, a gigantic stadium on the outskirts of the city. We grooved to electronic music, made memories while cementing our friendships. We had one great night after the next; Alfredo would introduce us to his friends, the deejays at the club who would play special music we would request. We slowly began to recognize people, and developed a nice local friends circle. Romans in general are a warm group of people. It was easy to be open and friendly and I learnt the merits of being active in an attempt to make the most of my study abroad experience. Upon gushing about my love for sweets one evening, our in-house Italian student resident, Alessia, volunteered to teach me how to make a tiramisu. Following it up, I bought the ingredients, set up a time that was mutually convenient and learnt how to make this decadent yet very simple desert. The effort of clearing my schedule one afternoon, making a few phone calls and a trip to the grocery store was well worth it! People who do not follow up on plans end up missing out on numerous unique learning opportunities.

The merits of general pro-activeness and leveraging a connection helped beyond my experience in Rome. As I travelled through different countries on the Semester at Sea program, I didn't hesitate to reach out to local friends for recommendations. When in Buenos Aires, I asked Guimar, an old UChicago acquaintance from Argentina for his input on where I should go to and fun things to do. Although he was abroad, he was unbelievably kind and introduced me to some of his friends in the city asking them to show me around. The best part about asking locals is that they are able to suggest places I would never be able to find as a tourist.

On my third night in Buenos Aires, three of my friends Dominique, Keller, Kirtee and I ended up going to a sushi restaurant. Now, there is nothing unique about a nice sushi restaurant, but this one had a secret bar in the back. Patrons needed a special password that they have to disclose to the waiter, and only then are they granted access. We were extremely curious about this and made our way to the chic Palermo Soho neighborhood dressed up with all sorts of expectations. As we arrived, we walked in with giggles wondering whether this was real. I took the lead, went in and asked for a table.

"I'm sorry," said the server. "The wait will be about one hour."

"Oh that's alright," I responded, "We can always have a drink at the bar in the meantime." As soon as I said this, I smiled and gave him the password for the secret bar. He looked at me, laughed, and asked where I was from. Given that I wasn't speaking an ounce of Spanish (seriously, I didn't even greet him with an 'hola') clearly I wasn't a local. He seemed startled that I knew the establishment had a secret bar, and looked very confused that I actually had the correct password.

"I'm from Mumbai, all the way in India. I'm only here for a few days. I've heard so much about the bar and my girl friends and I are very curious to try it. Please let us in." I finished with a confident look and dazzling smile. He smiled back and disappeared for a minute.

I saw him talk to the manager in the corner pointing at my friends and I. Two minutes later, he was guiding us to the back of the restaurant. We stepped into what resembled a storage room. He pushed a tarnished looking door that opened out into another room with a vault. He turned the knob on the vault and guided us into a little room with a few bookshelves. This was getting progressively mysterious and I felt as though I was an actress in some sort of suspense film. He stopped us before we could go any further and began narrating the story of the bar. Apparently it was run by a man whose father owned the restaurant up front. Decades ago, the son operated his own secret bar in the back for his friends to drink, people to make illegal bets and engage in other illegal activities. He finished off by saying that it continued to be the most secret bar of Buenos Aires (the identity, location and secret is still well kept) and therefore photography was prohibited. As we walked through the little room it opened up into yet another room with a few scattered tables. The final secret bar was situated right at the extreme back, which was a candlelit, intimate room with a piano in the corner. The place wasn't full at all, and there were a few affluent-looking locals. We were quite enamored as we watched the very limited gathering of folks in the bar and saw a lovely young couple cosying up in a corner. What a perfect place to bring a date! The exit door was separate from the entrance, and once one entered they'd have to exit through the exit door and re-enter using the password and traverse through multiple rooms. We were clearly the only tourists as majority wouldn't be aware that such a place existed.

The tables were arranged casually and we were greeted by friendly staff and a menu that was made to resemble the New York Times. We had a wonderful time consuming exclusive cocktails, mocktails and concoctions and simply taking in the ambience. We would have never known about this place if I hadn't taken the effort to connect with and ask an Argentine. I had a similarly wonderful experience learning from locals in Brazil, when Catarina introduced me to her friends Julia and Alex from Rio de Janeiro. I ended up staying with Julia's family for a few days, tasting wonderful local foods that her sister Luiza prepared and went out exploring the calm and collected vibes of Rio with Alex, Julia and their friend Barbara. I managed to gain meaningful interactions and a much richer perspective viewing Rio de Janeiro through a local lens. Once again, pro-activeness led to enhancing the nature of my experiences abroad.

Back home in Chicago, an outgoing personality and ability to leverage connections was advantageous. Driving, traffic and parking are perpetual problems in Chicago and owning a car can be more of a hassle than a convenience. Finding a reliable ride was a difficult task. As a result, my friends and I often took cabs into the downtown area, which was five-six miles north of campus against Lake Shore Drive. Thanks once again to Ada, I made a new friend. Mr. Rowland, aka Row was a taxi driver who once happened to be driving Ada and her roommates. Taxi drivers are interesting characters that often have a unique perspective of the city and its inhabitants, given that they drive people to and fro all day long. Ada enjoyed striking up a conversation with Row on the twenty-minute drive into the city. On discovering that he tended to drive customers in the Hyde Park area, Ada asked for his business card. From then on, whenever she needed a cab she would call Row who would promptly arrive to drive Ada and her roommates. They had created such a good rapport with him and employed his taxi so much that he willingly offered discounts and routinely charged a few dollars less than the reading on the meter. It was a win-win situation for everyone involved. Ada later referred him to me, and I was so pleasantly surprised at his promptness and passion - he was one happy taxi driver. I was also thrilled at how convenient life had become with a cabdriver friend at my beck and call, that I referred him to my sister Mehek and her friends. Row became a friend to us all, and would show up promptly whenever we required, driving us around at discounted rates. I'm so grateful to Ada for demonstrating to me the advantages of being social and being active in forming connections as in cases such as this, it had a domino effect in making my life easier - as well as that of my sister and our friends!

Being active also translates to the way in which one chooses to invest one's time. Fitting the most into a twenty-four hour day is essential as there is always something to do, and this time at college is a short phase in one's life. Being pro-active helped me attain novel and engaging opportunities such as the chance to work in a molecular gastronomy kitchen for one of the best chefs in the United States of America and spontaneously obtaining front row VIP seating with dignitaries of my college when Bill Gates came to address students.

Motivate yourself by remaining active. Feeling fulfilled will occur naturally if you center your college lifestyle around the key philosophies I have discussed in the book so far:

1. You have abundant potential - Don't put yourself in a box by allowing your capabilities to be defined by pre-determined categories.
2. Be positive - Consciously place focus on the appealing aspects that your new home offers.
3. Follow your passions and interests - Do not settle for something that makes you unhappy.
4. Make the small, daily choices count - Create life-affirming habits that enable you to become the best version of yourself.
5. Embrace changes and challenges - The ability to adapt to new people and places is a priceless trait, especially in our increasingly globalized world.
6. Study Abroad - Venture out of your social and/or geographic comfort zone if the opportunity permits. The personal growth and stories you create from these experiences are the treasures you will cherish the most in your life.

7. You are as powerful as your network - Be proactive in forming and maintaining connections. Networking will facilitate the accomplishment of your goals and often help you exceed them.

Lastly, I want to emphasize that happiness is a choice, a state of being. Irrespective of what you manage to do, looking at the glass half full, being grateful for what comes your way and taking a moment to pat yourself on the back for the things that you have achieved can go a long way. My philosophies for making the most of one's college experience is essentially grounded in this need to be happy, to be well. In a pursuit to race ahead, people often forget to remember how far they've come. Reflection and reminiscence is essential to inspire feelings of positive self-worth and to learn from one's mistakes moving forth. Leading a balanced and exciting life is great, but only if it brings you happiness internally. Chances are you probably won't achieve everything you want to do because time is limited and desires are many. Appreciating yourself for the things that you have managed to do is key - fuel your life with balance, follow your passions, make time for what is most important to you, broaden your perspectives through travel and diverse interaction, find beauty in one's immediate surroundings - these are some ways to bring about that happy state of being in college.

As I said to Armaan before, "Get ready for the best years of your life."

I'm certain that you will, in your own special way, make them sparkle.

The End

Connect with the author:

college.nehapremjee@gmail.com

twitter.com/nehapremjee

instagram.com/nehapremjee